CHAIRMAN'S NOTE

ALEXANDER FRIEDMAN

T he world has seemed to teeter on the edge of crisis throughout 2017.

Nationalist and populist politics dominated political debates, from the United States to the Philippines, and appear to presage a fundamental re-ordering of the institutions and norms that have driven international relations since World War II. President Donald Trump's administration is engulfed in growing scandal, fueling a sense of unease that is compounded by America's distancing of itself from the very global order it created.

Across the Atlantic, the UK appears to be headed toward a "hard" Brexit. Spain is facing down secessionism in Catalonia, its wealthiest region. And in Germany, like much of Europe, social democracy is ceding ground to a growing right-wing party. In the Middle East, Saudi Arabia is in the midst of a brutal bout of domestic political infighting, while the Kingdom's rivalry with Iran grows ever more tense. In Asia, the Korean Peninsula is a nuclear tinderbox, and China has become more autocratic than at any time in the last 40 years.

Natural disasters struck, too, in 2017. Consecutive hurricanes in the Atlantic devastated many small island states and territories in the Caribbean, powerful earthquakes killed hundreds in Mexico, monsoon floods displaced millions in South Asia, and huge fires burned across the American West. Yet these destructive environmental spasms are only the beginning of what will likely be an accelerating sequence of climate-related emergencies, unless humanity manages to take the collective steps necessary to slow the damage we have caused to our common home.

In the face of so many seemingly insurmountable challenges, it is tempting to adopt the expression of hopelessness and dread captured in Edvard Munch's famous painting "The Scream."

But, are the challenges facing us today really as unprecedented and potentially cataclysmic as they might seem? Or are we humans, limited by brief lifespans and even briefer attention spans, reflexively unable to put events into a broad enough context to see and learn from similar historical episodes?

This is where critical thinking and educated discourse come in and enable us, one hopes, to distinguish noise from substance – and thus to navigate today's conceptual uncertainty and political incoherence. And yet rarely has the public dissemination of ideas and facts been as threatened as it is now, whether from allegations of "fake news" in the interest of political expediency or from the manipulation of technological platforms that have replaced traditional news outlets without replicating their editorial standards.

Against this background, there has never been a more critical time for the work of *Project Syndicate*, which today stands alone as the only international source of original commentary from leading thinkers from every corner of the world – a global good that is needed now more than ever.

Only by putting experiences into historical and comparative perspective can we make effective decisions about our shared future. *The Year Ahead, 2018: Hope Against Rage* helps us do that. I trust you will enjoy and benefit from this important work.

Alexander Friedman
*Chief Executive Officer, GAM
Chairman, Advisory Board,
Project Syndicate*

Contents

50 Climate

66 Economics

EDITORS' INTRODUCTION

HOPE AGAINST RAGE

The world has entered what – for now at least – could be called a post-American epoch. During the first year of President Donald Trump's administration, the United States renounced its leadership role on a broad range of global issues, from trade to climate change, leaving the international order, and much of the world economy, in limbo.

Trump came to power in 2016 on a wave of populist rage, fueled by rapid social, economic, and technological change. Fortunately, in 2017, a more creative form of rage, born of hope rather than despair, could be glimpsed in many parts of the world, even within an angry and divided US. This emotional dichotomy is reflected throughout the following pages, in which some of the world's leading thinkers and policymakers examine what's come apart in the past year, and anticipate the forces and factors likely to define the year ahead.

The fundamental question is whether the international community can be reconfigured to address the most consequential policy challenges of our time. This is the question that former British Prime Minister Gordon Brown confronts head-on. He contends that reconfiguration is possible, but only if the international community can develop an entirely new paradigm to supplant a "leaderless" model of globalization that "lacks a human face, and advances like a runaway train careening out of control." The key, according to Brown, is to strike a balance between national sovereignty and local, regional, and international forms of governance. Failing that, he warns, "Protectionist and 'bring-back-control' movements will continue to flourish."

Pax...?

One of the most notable, if under-observed, developments of the first year of the Trump era was that trade arrangements and diplomatic relations already began to adjust to the new realities implied by a US intent on withdrawing from global engagement. Elmar Brok, who has twice chaired the foreign affairs committee of the European Parliament, notes that while Trump has brought about "negative, lasting change in the world order," America's partners have already started to "deepen their relationships with one another." In fact, toward the end of 2017, the European Union finalized a comprehensive trade deal with Japan.

Japan is also leading an effort to resurrect the Trans-Pacific Partnership, which Trump abandoned immediately after taking office. Former Australian Prime Minister Kevin Rudd sees the revived TPP taking shape among the 11 remaining Pacific-rim countries as a "significant advance in terms of trade and investment." But he worries that, more broadly, America's abdication of international leadership has left the "global trading system utterly rudderless," and handed the strategic advantage in Asia to China. The same applies to Trump's thoughtless attempts to resolve the nuclear standoff with North Korea.

But Yuriko Koike, the Governor of Tokyo, identifies a novel way to address such problems in a post-American world – and one in keeping with the type of reconfiguration Brown has in mind. For Koike, "the beating cultural heart of modern Asian societies" are its megacities, such as Tokyo and Seoul, whose leaders can work with their national governments and one another to confront shared threats.

In 2017, the biggest threat of all was posed by Kim Jong-un's regime in North Korea, which spent the year in a war of words with Trump, while making further progress toward developing an intercontinental ballistic missile capable of delivering a nuclear strike against the US mainland. "No city is an island, safe unto itself," says Koike. "That is why the leaders of Asia's megacities should be fighting for policies that will help to neutralize the threat to the entire region, not just our own homes."

But, whereas Koike envisions a distributed, transnational network of urban leaders, China moved in the opposite direction in 2017, toward greater centralization of authority. At the 19th National Congress of the Communist Party of China in October, President Xi Jinping became the most powerful Chinese leader since Mao Zedong. Still, Minxin Pei of Claremont McKenna College calls into question the viability of Xi's approach. With or without "significantly augmented power," Pei notes, Xi's bid for global economic leadership is far from guaranteed, in part because he faces pervasive "passive resistance" within the CPC, whose members cannot honestly "believe that their country's future lies in a centralized, fear-based authoritarian regime."

Democracy on the Ropes

In addition to global realignments, 2017 was another year of what Indian-American anthropologist Arjun Appadurai has called "democratic fatigue." The Trump administration, in addition to pursuing illiberal policies against immigrants and minority groups at home, has ushered in a state

of exception abroad. Abuses by American allies and partners that once would have invited rebuke from the US no longer do. In 2017, the governments of Vietnam, Egypt, the Philippines, Saudi Arabia, Poland, Turkey, and other countries carried out extrajudicial killings, undermined democratic institutions, attacked the media, or otherwise violated their citizens' rights, all with the Trump administration's tacit support or, worse, its explicit approval.

On the few occasions that Trump did address other governments' actions, he made matters worse. In addition to goading the already paranoid North Korean regime, he also emboldened Iran's hardliners and undermined its reform-minded president by refusing to recertify the 2015 Iran nuclear deal. And, as former Mexican Foreign Minister Jorge G. Castañeda observes, Trump's threat of US military intervention in Venezuela may have "torpedoed any chance of a speedy resolution" of a crisis pitting President Nicolás Maduro's thuggish, kleptocratic regime against opposition protesters who took to the streets throughout the year.

For her part, María Corina Machado of Súmante, a Caracas-based election-monitoring organization, laments that the international community did almost nothing in 2017 to support Venezuela's democratic opposition. She notes that, while the Venezuelan people literally starve, the Maduro regime is supporting drug cartels, money launderers, arms traffickers, and other non-state actors that pose a threat to all countries.

Beyond Venezuela's political-cum-humanitarian tragedy, the world's democracies failed to marshal an adequate response to serious violations of international norms elsewhere. In Myanmar, for example, the democratically elected government of Aung San Suu Kyi has by turns denied, minimized, and excused the military's brutal ethnic-cleansing campaign against the country's Rohingya Muslims. As a result, a crisis that had been confined to Myanmar's Rakhine State has now overburdened neighboring Bangladesh with a flood of refugees.

The increasingly apparent inability of the world's democracies to mount effective responses to crises abroad at least partly reflects a different sort of crisis at home. ➔

> **The world still has a choice – and in 2017 it appeared determined to make the right one.**

1:
XI JINPING AND
VLADIMIR PUTIN.

Former British Prime Minister Tony Blair argues that democracies, particularly in the West, have become dysfunctional for lack of a "center ground." With the right "fissuring" between nationalists and free-market liberals, and the left "also dividing" into "statist" and more "mainstream" camps, extreme polarization has rendered democratic governance ineffective, and thus increasingly unappealing to voters.

Former Polish Foreign Minister Radosław Sikorski attributes today's political realignments to "citizens' alienation from an establishment that has failed or is unable to respond to some salient challenge." But Sikorski finds hope by looking to history. After all, the illiberal populism we see today in Europe, the US, and elsewhere is not a new phenomenon. Cooptation is key: "Wise establishmentarians accommodate some populist arguments within their own political programs," Sikorski notes. "After these concessions are made, emotions tend to cool, and social stability can be restored." But while many had hoped that French President Emmanuel Macron and German Chancellor Angela Merkel would lead precisely such an accommodation in 2018, the political uncertainty that has engulfed Germany since the federal election in September suggests that the "establishmentarians" may be too fragmented to pull it off.

Janine R. Wedel of George Mason University offers an additional explanation for contemporary populist "revolts": violations of the public trust, which can lead citizens to seek out radical leadership alternatives. In the past year and a half alone, Wedel observes, corruption and official-misconduct scandals toppled Brazilian President Dilma Rousseff, South Korean President Park Geun-hye, Pakistani Prime Minister Nawaz Sharif, and US Secretary of Health and Human Services Tom Price. But, complicating matters further, in 2017, anti-corruption campaigns – "draining the swamp" – became a favored tool for consolidating power among strongmen, from Xi and Trump to Turkish President Recep Tayyip Erdoğan and Saudi Crown Prince Mohammed bin Salman.

Samantha Bradshaw and Philip N. Howard of Oxford University identify yet another culprit behind declining trust: social media companies such as Facebook, Google, and Twitter, which continued to inundate voters with misinformation throughout 2017. In 2016, Russia used the major social-media platforms to meddle in the United Kingdom's Brexit referendum and the US presidential election; in 2017, it did so again – albeit with less success – in elections in France, Germany, the Netherlands, and the UK. "If democracy is to survive," Bradshaw and Howard conclude, "today's social media giants will have to redesign themselves."

Raging Storms and Rays of Sun

The stakes could not be higher, because the future of humanity depends on the close international cooperation that the global spread of democracy has enabled. In 2017, atmospheric carbon dioxide reached its highest level in three million years, and flooding, droughts, wildfires, and other extreme weather and weather-related events continued to increase in frequency and severity. And, together with the post-American realignment and the trials of liberal democracy, climate action in 2017 became a source of deep uncertainty.

But the world still has a choice – and in 2017 it appeared determined to make the right one. As Laurence Tubiana of the European Climate Foundation points out, by the time Trump followed through on his campaign promise to "cancel" the 2015 Paris climate accord, the rest of the world was already forging ahead without the US. Equally important, as a truly global problem, climate change has given rise to the kind of hybrid leadership model that Brown and Koike describe. At the United Nations Climate Change Conference in Bonn in November, the official US delegations from the White House and the Department of State were overshadowed by a delegation of US governors and urban, business, and civil-society leaders reaffirming American commitments to the Paris accord.

Like the American shadow delegation in Bonn, the world's international financial institutions have also come together voluntarily to take action. In the essay "A Truly Global Response to Climate Change," the leaders of the world's nine major development banks offer a plan for "aligning financial flows to the Paris agreement." They remind us that while climate change poses an existential threat, it also presents an opportunity for "development and poverty reduction all over the world."

Hope, tempered by caution, also characterized the global economy in 2017.

Nobel laureate economist Edmund S. Phelps also touts the opportunities of moving to a clean-energy economy based on sustainable growth. But he warns that unless the relevant incentives are changed, businesses will not reduce emissions – let alone develop the technologies needed to extract CO_2 from the atmosphere – at anywhere near the scale needed to prevent catastrophic climate change in the coming decades. If sound leadership does prevail, he envisions a future in which mankind has revived "an older conception of work based on exercising one's initiative and using one's creativity" in the interest of the planet. Quoting Abraham Lincoln, Phelps hopes that twenty-first-century societies can reacquaint themselves with "a great passion – a perfect rage – for the 'new'."

Risks and Unshared Rewards

Hope, tempered by caution, also characterized the global economy in 2017. As Nobel laureate economist Joseph E. Stiglitz observes, "the decade-long recovery from the Great Recession is *finally* taking hold." Still, he warns of "large risks on the horizon." In the US, protectionism or debt-fueled stimulus could undermine growth in the long term – and invite an interest-rate hike and market correction in the near term.

In the UK – where Prime Minister Theresa May initiated in March the formal process for withdrawal from the EU, and then lost her Conservative Party's parliamentary majority in a snap election in June – the full costs of Brexit are only starting to be seen. If the government cannot make more progress in its exit negotiations with the EU in 2018, it may find itself crashing out of the European single market and customs union in 2019. And in China, Stiglitz notes, the government will have to manage the risks of its "complicated transition from export-led growth to growth driven by domestic demand."

Likewise, International Monetary Fund Chief Economist Maurice Obstfeld is relatively bullish on near-term growth, but worries about the longer term. "Aging workforces, slower productivity growth, and higher debt burdens since the crisis darken the outlook," he argues, ➔

> **Even barring another downturn, the current recovery has largely failed to benefit most workers.**

particularly in advanced economies. In fact, former US Secretary of the Treasury Lawrence H. Summers puts "the annual probability of recession in the coming years at 20-25%," owing not least to "highly problematic economic leadership in the Trump administration." Moreover, Summers worries that the next downturn "may well be protracted and deep, with severe global consequences," because "the traditional strategy for battling recession – a reduction of 500 basis points in the federal funds rate – will be unavailable this year, given the zero lower bound on interest rates."

Alexander Friedman of the investment management firm GAM cautions that monetary policy itself may have already sown the seeds of the next recession. Ultra-low interest rates, quantitative easing (QE), and other unconventional policies that have fueled risk assets over the past decade now have to be unwound. "If managing the financial crisis and rolling out unprecedented policies seemed difficult," he writes, "just wait for what has to come next: withdrawal of unprecedented levels of liquidity from the economy."

Even barring another downturn, the current recovery has largely failed to benefit most workers, which helps to explain why populist movements emerged during one of the longest recoveries on record. Nobel laureate economist Angus Deaton points out that while "median real (inflation-adjusted) wages in the US have stagnated over the past 50 years," there is growing evidence to suggest that the "rich are getting richer at the expense of everyone else." According to Deaton, health-care costs, market consolidation, changing employment patterns, and inadequate regulation have allowed the

wealthy to "capture" for themselves most of the gains of the past few decades. Still, he is hopeful. If today's maldistribution of wealth is not an "irremediable consequence of unstoppable processes such as globalization and technological change," then it can be addressed with the right policies.

The Future of Leadership

As Brown reminds us, achieving more equitable growth will depend on balancing national policymaking with international cooperation. Western wage stagnation, for example, cannot be reversed without ending the "race to the bottom in labor standards" in some African and Asian countries. To that end, developing countries can take inspiration from Indonesia, which, according to its finance minister, Sri Mulyani Indrawati, "is experiencing solid growth in new jobs and real wages." Indrawati shows that President Joko Widodo's government has managed to gain the trust of Indonesians and foreign investors alike, by making substantial investments in education, skills-training, and infrastructure.

Célestin Monga, Chief Economist of the African Development Bank, notes that many African countries also boast huge potential for inclusive growth. The problem is that "only a fraction of global foreign direct investment (FDI) flows ... are likely to go to Africa." Without multilateral leadership and a better framework for "channeling excess savings from the global North into profitable investment opportunities in the global South," he warns, shared problems such

1:
DONALD TRUMP.

2:
FRANKLIN D. ROOSEVELT.

Central bankers need to do a better job of managing the public's expectations; but so do politicians.

as mass migration into Europe and elsewhere will persist.

Raghuram G. Rajan of the University of Chicago points out that monetary policies in advanced economies add another layer of interdependency. When monetary policy in these countries is loose, yield-seeking investors pour into emerging economies, only to flee *en masse* when policy is tightened. More broadly, Rajan thinks that central bankers urgently need to come to terms with the ever-expanding role they have assumed in national and international economic governance over the past decade.

On one hand, Rajan notes, central banks were right to "go to great lengths to stabilize financial markets" during the worst downturn since the Great Depression. On the other hand, they have become "prisoners of their inflation-targeting mandate." Inflation targets, Rajan points out, became the main anchor for monetary policy at a time when central bankers "were really focused on the upper limit," and few imagined that they would "be struggling to move inflation up into the band rather than down into it." In today's context of stubbornly low inflation, policymakers have become "trapped by a mandate they do not necessarily know how to achieve." Rajan hopes that central banks will use 2018 to conduct a "sober assessment of their policies over the last few years," and to clarify their mandate and operational remit.

Central bankers need to do a better job of managing the public's expectations; but so do politicians. Jason Furman, who served as Chairman of the US Council of Economic Advisers under President Barack Obama, shares a hard truth: no public policy can overcome

"concerns with inequality and slow income growth" in advanced economies. Although measures to improve access to education and employment are certainly justified, they will not reverse "deep factors, like demographic trends and slow productivity growth worldwide." Lying about what your policies can achieve is a luxury reserved for populists. The task for responsible leaders, Furman emphasizes, is to find "better ways to communicate about the challenges we face, the efforts being made to address them, and the inherent limits that confront all policymakers."

Mariana Mazzucato of University College London, on the other hand, hopes that policymakers can overcome some of those limits by shedding orthodox *laissez-faire* assumptions about the role of the state in the economy. During the post-war period, she reminds us, the US government funded mission-oriented institutions like NASA and DARPA (the Defense Advanced Research Projects Agency), which laid the groundwork for what would become the Internet. In recent decades, however, civil servants have gone from being "market creators" to mere "market fixers," to the detriment of the public and private sectors alike.

Klaus Schwab, Founder and Chairman of the World Economic Forum, also envisions a more dynamic form of policymaking, whereby government becomes as "agile" as cutting-edge companies. The public sector should "heed the lessons of the technology sector," he argues, "where a start-up that is not prepared to pivot when necessary won't be around for long." For Schwab, the key to governance in the twenty-first century is a willingness to "adapt, explore, learn, and adjust endlessly."

That is an imperative that captures the single most important message of the essays gathered here: Managing rapid, far-reaching economic change and geopolitical shifts, while preserving hard-won democratic institutions, will require what Franklin D. Roosevelt famously called "bold, persistent experimentation." At the height of the Great Depression, with democracy in retreat and fascism ascendant in Europe, Roosevelt called for leadership based on "enthusiasm, imagination, and the ability to face facts, even unpleasant ones, bravely." Such leadership certainly will not come from the US in 2018. But a post-American world, or the restoration of US leadership, will demand nothing less. **PS**

Roman Frydman
Kenneth Murphy
Jonathan Stein
Stuart Whatley

A NEW BALANCE

FOR THE GLOBAL

AGE

GORDON BROWN
Former British Prime Minister

Protectionist and "bring-back-control" movements will continue to flourish so long as globalization remains leaderless, lacks a human face, and advances like a runaway train careening out of control.

1.

Sadly, there are good reasons why globalization has become a dirty word for millions of people. The pillars of the 30-year-old Washington Consensus have been collapsing. Most now agree that free trade without fair trade creates millions of losers, in addition to some winners. Unregulated capital flows, especially short-term speculative flows, can destabilize economies. And rising social inequalities can be bad for growth.

These realizations are punching holes in the free-market fundamentalism – focused on liberalization, deregulation, privatization, tax-cutting, and the shrinking of the state – that has prevailed in policymaking circles over the last few decades. Ten years after the global financial crisis, we can now accept that individuals and corporations acting solely in their own self-interest do not always serve that of the public.

And yet a new economic paradigm for the global age still has not emerged. In the resulting vacuum, protectionism, anti-trade populism, and illiberal – often xenophobic – nationalism have gained ground, fueled by anxieties about stagnant wages, technological unemployment, and rising insecurity. Make no mistake: those left out and left behind by globalization are actively searching for something and someone to articulate their discontent and shelter them from change.

But neither nationalism – whether that espoused by US President Donald Trump or its other manifestations – nor overly formulaic or elaborate systems of global governance will meet the needs and desires of people for prosperity, security, equity, and self-determination. The former fails to confront the realities of a world where our independence is limited by our interdependence; the latter runs counter to a strong current in public opinion favoring more local control.

If we are to tame globalization and respect national identities, we must strike the right balance between the national autonomy most citizens desire and the international agreements most countries so patently need.

Trump's "America First" nationalism proposes to cut imports, restrict immigration, and withdraw the US from the Paris climate agreement, international organizations like UNESCO, and free-trade deals. For a country that benefits hugely from its leading role in global supply chains, this is a self-defeating strategy.

Trump doesn't know – or perhaps doesn't want to know – that cutting imports threatens to cut exports, because billions of dollars in US exports rely on imported components. He forgets that the profitability of many US corporations depends more on Asian workers using American technology than on more expensive American workers using the same production techniques. These companies will fight any attempts to limit their access to global supply chains.

The progressive alternative that is usually advanced – "responsible nationalism" – is essentially a program to compensate the squeezed middle classes through re-training and wage subsidies. But even professedly generous European welfare systems lift no more than one-third of the poor out of poverty.

In the US, inequalities are now so glaring that the federal earned income tax credit provides only 2.5% of what would be needed to restore the distribution of income between the bottom 80% and top 20% to 1980s levels. Former US Secretary of the Treasury Lawrence H. Summers has calculated that the top 1% would be required to pay $1 trillion extra in tax ($700,000 each) per year to close the gap that has emerged.

Addressing high levels of inequality will almost certainly require international cooperation to repatriate billions from tax havens. And even then, we would still have to deal with Asian and African countries out-competing the West on price, because of a race to the bottom in labor standards – a root cause of Western wage stagnation.

The battle against environmental degradation poses the same problem: sustainable progress against pollution cannot be made if nation-states fail to take seriously their responsibilities to reduce carbon dioxide emissions and switch to renewable energy. Yet, without concerted international action to force free riders into line, pollution will cross borders, and environmental damage will spread and multiply.

So there is a limit to national-level solutions. While it is sensible to oppose the wrong kind of global cooperation, the right kind of cooperation is vital to achieve national prosperity in this hyper-connected era. With market power still expanding at the expense of governments, policies focused exclusively on pulling the levers of the nation-state will fail to deal

2.

not just with pollution and inequality, but also with macroeconomic imbalances, beggar-thy-neighbor trade policies and their spillover effects, cyber attacks, and pandemics – each of which now poses a transnational problem that requires an international response.

Striking the right balance between autonomy and cooperation comes down to being clear about the distinction between nineteenth- and twenty-first-century concepts of state sovereignty. In the former, power is centralized, held by a single state that is seen as indivisible; the latter is focused on popular self-government, with citizens making their own democratic choices about whether power resides locally, nationally, or internationally.

In some areas, citizens will choose their national government as sole decision-maker. In others, they may choose to share decision-making power in regional blocs like the European Union or in international organizations, such as the United Nations and NATO, that agree to share responsibilities, resources, and risks.

Getting the balance right is the unstated issue at the heart of the argument not just about the limits and extent of

global cooperation, but also, and more immediately, about the future of the UK's relationship with the EU. Reflexive reactions like Brexit, America First-style strategies, and overly intricate frameworks of supranational governance are all inadequate to satisfy the modern world's imperatives to cooperate across borders and to uphold the pride people have in their distinctive national identities.

Striking the balance between national independence and cross-national cooperation will more likely be achieved on an issue-by-issue basis, and the boundaries will shift as the world economy and popular opinion change.

Harvard University economist Dani Rodrik, whose writings expose the weaknesses of neoliberal globalization, suggests that, in some areas, we should be expanding or consolidating the nation-state's power. Such an approach would recognize, for example, domestic preferences when it comes to food- and product-safety standards, or the need to moderate so-called Investor-State Dispute Settlement processes, which are frequently criticized for undercutting domestic laws. ➔

1:
A CHILD IN GLASGOW, SCOTLAND.

2:
G20 CONFERENCE, 2017.

1.

2.

National governments must also recognize the value of self-imposed restrictions on excessive deficits and surpluses, and resist currency manipulation. But macroeconomic imbalances may be best reduced by reciprocal, cooperative agreements.

Of course, nation-states will want to make their own tax decisions to suit local cultures and circumstances. But a failure to cooperate to tackle unfair tax competition and to close down offshore tax havens will irrevocably damage every country's revenue base and its domestic plans for spending on education, health care, and security.

In 2018 and beyond, we should establish realistic plans for responding to the backlash against globalization by managing globalization better. No one has a complete roadmap for balancing national autonomy and international cooperation. But the best way to begin is to focus international cooperative efforts on areas where the benefits are greatest, or the costs of non-cooperation are the highest. But we will also have to deal directly and forthrightly with distributional questions, whether in trade, climate change, investment, or the development and deployment of technologies.

First, it is time to create a worldwide early warning system for financial markets that is based on globally applicable standards for capital adequacy, liquidity, transparency, and accountability, and includes agreed trigger points for action when risks multiply. For example, New York University economist Roman Frydman has proposed a mechanism to impose a ceiling on new debt creation when asset prices escalate too quickly.

1:
GORDON BROWN SPEAKING
AT BIRMINGHAM UNIVERSITY.

2:
A HOMELESS MAN IN
NEW YORK.

With America in retreat and Brexit threatening to isolate Britain, 2018 will almost certainly have setbacks.

More broadly, we need to expand the scope of post-crisis financial-restructuring efforts to cover all global financial centers. Otherwise, when the next crisis hits, we will still not know what is owned or owed by whom, where, and on what basis. Critics will be right in asking why we failed to learn from the 2008 financial crisis.

Second, we need to reform global supply and value chains. Of course we should have fair intellectual-property, tariff, and non-tariff rules. But we must also address the fundamental injustices that are at the heart of global supply chains, fueling today's anti-globalization protests. Intelligent reform of global supply chains should stamp out environmental free riders; reverse the current race to the bottom in labor markets; curtail trafficking and money laundering; eliminate transfer-pricing and tax-avoidance schemes that allow for goods to be taxed – at a lower rate – in countries they never enter; and shut down the tax havens that now hold trillions of dollars.

Third, we need to improve macroeconomic cooperation. For the past decade, growth in global output and trade have been much lower than they should and could have been. Proposals such as the G20 Mutual Assessment Process (MAP) and the International Monetary Fund's "imbalances" initiative have made only token progress.

In 2009, I proposed a nominal growth target for the world economy, as a way to secure a faster recovery from the post-crisis recession. Then, in 2010, the G20 reached an agreement under which major exporting countries such as China would limit their current-account surpluses to 4%, and major importing countries such as the US would cap their deficits.

Robert Skidelsky of Warwick University recently updated this Keynesian idea with a detailed proposal requiring both creditors and debtors to make adjustments wherever imbalances arise. And Nobel laureate economist Joseph E. Stiglitz has called for an IMF scheme to insure emerging countries against risk, thereby freeing them from having to hold excessive reserves, which are unproductive in normal times.

Generally speaking, reducing macroeconomic imbalances and boosting growth will require a stronger G20. The premier forum for economic cooperation should have an executive capacity and a broader and more representative membership.

When I was prime minister of the United Kingdom, the British government fought hard for a world trade deal, while India and America remained at loggerheads over curbing agriculture imports to protect Indian farmers' livelihoods. Today, without America's help, Pacific-rim countries are discussing their own multilateral trade deals, which suggests that we should be planning for a time, post-Trump, when a new world trade deal might be possible once again.

In the meantime, as Nobel laureate economist Michael Spence has eloquently argued, the IMF should be intensifying its focus on global surveillance, in order to identify and remove structural weaknesses in a fast-changing world economy.

It would also help if plans for financing the UN Sustainable Development Goals for 2030 included recapitalizing the World Bank to give it more borrowing power. The Bank's resources could be increased substantially by merging its low-income-country fund, the

International Development Association, with its middle-income-country fund, the International Bank for Reconstruction and Development, and by encouraging more cooperation between it and other regional development banks.

As participants discussed at the pioneering Billions to Trillions forum in Addis Ababa, Ethiopia, almost three years ago, development targets for the environment, health, gender equality, and employment call for innovative delivery plans to make the best use of the world's $160 billion aid budget. The International Commission on Financing Global Education Opportunity, which I chaired, has proposed a private-public financing facility that could complement existing institutions and raise an additional $10 billion annually for education worldwide.

More to the point, we must develop mechanisms that go beyond simply holding out a begging bowl. Only through innovation can we adequately provide for the world's 20 million refugees and 60 million displaced people, who have suffered untold atrocities, and whom the UN, under Secretary-General António Guterres, is working so hard to help.

It is right for the international community to set ambitious development goals. But our failure to deliver on those goals will invite charges of betrayal. Nationalists will continue to argue that mainstream leaders cannot be trusted, and extremists of all stripes will insist that coexistence among countries, cultures, and religions is impossible.

With America in retreat and Brexit threatening to isolate Britain, 2018 will almost certainly have setbacks. But waiting in the wings is a new agenda that can ensure prosperity for all countries, not just through national actions, but also through enhanced international cooperation, starting in the areas with the most promise, and then spreading across the board. PS

***Gordon Brown**, former Prime Minister and Chancellor of the Exchequer of the United Kingdom, is United Nations Special Envoy for Global Education and Chair of the International Commission on Financing Global Education Opportunity, and the author of* My Life, Our Times. *He chairs the Advisory Board of the Catalyst Foundation.*

It's Not E It's Me...

"America First" Wakes Up the EU

ELMAR BROK
Former Chairman of the Committee on Foreign Affairs, European Parliament

US President Donald Trump has been in office for less than a year, but he has already put the relationship between Europe and the United States to the test. Be it defense and security cooperation within NATO, trade relations, cooperation on global challenges like climate change, or participation in bodies such as the G7 or G20, there is hardly any area that has not been adversely affected by Trump's malign judgment.

For over a century, the transatlantic partnership has been central to US foreign policy. At a time when the key challenges we face – from terrorism to climate change to mass migration – extend far beyond national borders, such cooperation is more important than ever.

Yet Trump's "America First" approach, together with his erratic leadership style, is undermining the partnerships and mutual agreements on which transatlantic – and, indeed, global – cooperation has long been based. Trump's doctrine might please his core constituents, but it fails to account for even the most basic principles and mechanisms of international politics.

For all his supposed "deal-making" skills, Trump seems not to understand that international agreements work only if they benefit all parties – and that this demands compromise. As a result, he is taking actions that jeopardize the cohesion and unity of the West, while bringing about negative, lasting change in the world order. Trump's approach to defense, trade, and climate change are emblematic of this pattern.

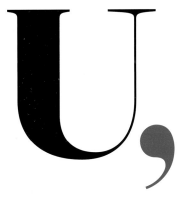

A strong NATO is undoubtedly in the interest of both the US and the European Union. That is why Trump's often-misleading criticisms of the Alliance, which cast doubt on his loyalty to it, were so dangerous. Though Trump eventually endorsed Article 5 of the North Atlantic Treaty – the mutual-defense commitment that forms the core of NATO – the damage was done.

As a result, the West is widely perceived – including by world leaders – to be divided and weak. Russian President Vladimir Putin, for one, has taken this as a sign that he can continue to challenge openly the European and global security architecture.

In recent years, Putin has attempted to facilitate his violations of the sovereignty and territorial integrity of neighboring countries by undermining the cohesion of the EU and NATO, whether through disinformation campaigns or by providing financial support to Euroskeptic and fascist groups in Europe. In this sense, Trump's equivocation about NATO has played directly into Putin's hands.

The good news is that the EU seems to understand that, if it can't rely on the US, it needs to take matters into its own hands, by pursuing more integrated security and defense policies. Last June, EU leaders agreed to activate the "Permanent Structured Cooperation" (PESCO), which allows the bloc to implement joint defense projects that strengthen its overall defense capabilities.

We will take further concrete steps to improve cooperation among European armed forces. Collectively, European armies have more soldiers than the US and spend more on defense than Russia or China. But their efficiency is equivalent to just 10-15% that of the US. Analysts estimate that the lack of effective defense cooperation among EU member states costs up to €100 billion ($116 billion) annually. Given this, increasing cooperation could not be more important, though European defensive capabilities will be a complement to NATO, not a replacement.

Another policy that could undermine transatlantic security – both directly, and by further distancing the US from its allies – is Trump's decertification of the Iran nuclear deal. Although the deal doesn't directly address many aspects of Iran's destabilizing behavior, especially its threats toward Israel, the EU – and the entire international community – remain convinced that the agreement is needed in order to enable constructive engagement with Iran in those areas.

As for trade, Trump's suspicion and even rejection of international trade agreements has created a large political vacuum that others – especially China – will seek to fill. As Trump continues to tout his nationalist approach to trade, America's partners are looking to deepen their relationships with one another. The recent trade deal between the EU – which accounts for more world trade than China and the US combined – and Japan will be the world's largest.

The geostrategic implications of this trend should not be underestimated. If Trump continues on the path toward protectionism, America's trading partners will retaliate. Any US actions against EU steel exports, for example, would certainly trigger a prompt reprisal from the EU. And trade conflicts would surely affect relations in other areas.

Then there is issue of climate change. Trump has withdrawn the US from the 2015 Paris climate agreement. By contrast, the EU considers climate action to be one of its top priorities, not just for the obvious ecological, social, and economic reasons, but also to support a comprehensive foreign and security policy. After all, unbridled climate change will inevitably trigger destabilizing mass migration, particularly from climate-vulnerable regions like Africa.

Given that the US is the world's largest polluter in history, Trump's pursuit of climate-destroying policies, including his support for the American coal and cement industries, will have global implications. And, contrary to Trump's rhetoric, it will undermine America's own future competitiveness. Unsurprisingly, future-oriented US companies like Tesla oppose this dangerous policy orientation.

The EU must recognize that the US will not be as reliable a partner in the coming years as it has been since the end of World War II, and it must adjust accordingly. Of course, Trump won't be president forever, and the ties that bind the US and Europe will outlast him. The EU and the US remain each other's most important economic and security partners, and this fact is likely to bring the two sides back together once Trump's tenure is over. In the meantime, however, the EU needs to do what it takes to protect its own interests on the world stage – with or without the US. PS

***Elmar Brok**, a former chairman of the Committee on Foreign Affairs in the European Parliament, is a senior official of Germany's Christian Democratic Union.*

The Trumping of Asia

KEVIN RUDD
Former Prime Minister of Australia

I n the last year, the single most pointless wound inflicted by the US on Asia, not to mention itself, was its abandonment of the Trans-Pacific Partnership. In one fell swoop, the once great free-trading nation that was the United States of America died, leaving the global trading system utterly rudderless.

With America's spurning of the TPP, not only was progress toward further trade liberalization reversed; the global free-trade system itself, including its common rules and arbitration mechanisms for resolving disputes, came into question.

You don't have to be a Marxist to understand that economics has a profound and probably even decisive impact on politics, both national and international. And, indeed, the geopolitical and geo-economic implications of Trump's move are just beginning to be felt across the Pacific.

With China's economic footprint across the Asia-Pacific region already large, countries in the region are now increasingly concluding that the US is consigning itself to growing economic irrelevance in Asia. US financial institutions will, of course, remain important, as will Silicon Valley, as a source of extraordinary innovation. But the pattern of trade, the direction of investment, and, increasingly, the nature of intra-regional capital flows, are painting a vastly different picture for the future than the one that has dominated post-war Asia.

The abandonment of the TPP – a key campaign promise that Donald Trump fulfilled almost immediately upon taking office – reflects the collective failure on the part of the American political class in the 2016 presidential election. Continuing that failure, America's leadership has not followed up on the decision with much of anything.

At home, the Trump administration has engaged in much chest-thumping about "America First." Abroad, it has begun to tout an ill-defined concept of "a free and open Indo-Pacific," which displays all the hallmarks of a slogan in search of substance. What economic reality will hang beneath this shingle, we know not. If the idea is a series of individual bilateral free-trade agreements, any seasoned observer of US trade diplomacy can tell you that we are looking at a decade's worth of negotiations that, ultimately, will probably yield very little.

For their part, Asia-Pacific countries have begun to look to two unlikely sources for leadership on trade liberalization: Japan and China.

Japan has sought to pull the TPP's remains out of the ashes by creating the TPP 11, which includes all of the original negotiating states, except the US, which would be permitted to rejoin later. The core tenets of this agreement were signed, despite reservations from Canada, at the November Asia-Pacific Economic Cooperation (APEC) summit in Da Nang, Vietnam (a meeting that Trump himself also attended), highlighting Asia-Pacific countries' view that they are no longer chained to US leadership. The so-called Comprehensive and Progressive Trans-Pacific Partnership represents a significant advance in terms of trade and investment liberalization across the 11 signatory countries. As for the US, we can only hope that a future administration, whether Republican or Democrat, will see its way clear to acceding to an agreement that Japanese economic leadership has sought to keep alive. But, given the evidence, that may be farfetched.

The other surprising source of trade leadership in the Asia-Pacific region is China. Some years ago, the country began championing a Regional Comprehensive Economic Partnership (RCEP). While this will not represent a high-ambition arrangement, it will represent some advancement from the *status quo*. It embraces 16 states, including China, India, Japan, and South Korea, but excludes the US.

India, the third-largest economy in Asia, could also have a critical role to play in furthering pan-regional trade liberalization. But Prime Minister Narendra Modi's government has yet to direct its political capital toward becoming a member of APEC, let alone advance a trade-liberalization agenda of its own. This needs to change, but the forces of mercantilism are alive and well in Delhi.

The net result of these developments, with the US having eschewed both the TPP and RCEP, has been a further diminution of American power in the Asia-Pacific region. In fact, the US is increasingly emerging as an incomplete superpower. It remains a formidable military actor, with unique power projection capabilities that extend far beyond its aircraft carrier battle groups to include an array of other capabilities that are as yet unmatched by other countries in the Asia-Pacific region. But its relevance to the region's future – in terms of employment, trade, and investment growth, as well as sustainable development – is declining fast.

Some in Washington, DC, seem to think that the US can sustain this pattern for decades to come. But many of us are skeptical. Unless and until the US chooses comprehensive economic re-engagement with the region, its significance to the overall future of Asia, the world's most economically dynamic region, will continue to fade.

Precisely how other regional powers – China, Japan, India, and South Korea (Asia's four leading economies) – will respond to this decline remains to be seen. But the truth confronting those who observe the region closely is that Southeast Asia has already begun to move meaningfully toward China's strategic orbit.

Ultimately, the policies of an administration committed to putting America first are likely, in Asia at least, to result in America being put last. **PS**

Kevin Rudd, *a former Prime Minister of Australia, is President of the Asia Society Policy Institute in New York and Chair of the Independent Commission on Multilateralism.*

Asia's Cities Against North Korea

YURIKO KOIKE
Governor of Tokyo

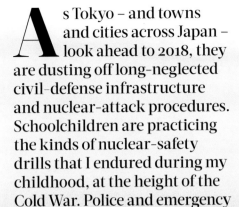

As Tokyo – and towns and cities across Japan – look ahead to 2018, they are dusting off long-neglected civil-defense infrastructure and nuclear-attack procedures. Schoolchildren are practicing the kinds of nuclear-safety drills that I endured during my childhood, at the height of the Cold War. Police and emergency first responders are brushing up on measures that had fallen into disuse since the 1990s. Hospitals are undergoing stress tests of their readiness. Fallout shelters are being inspected and restored. And the potential of new innovations and resources to reinforce civilians' security is being explored. ➲

29日・　前6時前　　道弾1発を発射
襟裳　　　　を通過　　平洋上に落下か

Much of this preparation – spurred by North Korea's increasing belligerence, including launches of missiles over Japan – is occurring on the local level. And, beyond Japan, plenty of other Asian cities are pursuing similar initiatives to strengthen their civil defense. But cities can do more than lead the way in emergency-response preparedness; we can – and therefore must – play a central role in helping to avoid conflict and defuse tensions.

Like Tokyo's governors during the Cold War, I do not believe that we will actually face the horrors of a nuclear attack. But when it comes to the safety and wellbeing of Tokyo's citizens, my government and the agencies that it directs can never be too careful – or too ready. Anything less than our best efforts at preparedness would not only be reckless; it would also be an insult to the memory of those who died in the nuclear firestorms that followed the bombing of Hiroshima and Nagasaki in 1945.

Despite Japan's uniquely intimate history with nuclear attacks, this vigilance is not limited to my country, much less to Tokyo. Though Tokyo is my primary responsibility, and the focus of all my thoughts and plans, I am also concerned with the fate of the capital of next-door South Korea, Tokyo's great sister city.

I know the Korean people well, and I have no doubt that they, too, are preparing with their characteristic rigor and stoicism. Yet Seoul remains particularly vulnerable to the whims of North Korea's impetuous and ruthless leader, Kim Jong-un – and that should concern all of Asia's municipal leaders.

No city is an island, safe unto itself. That is why the leaders of Asia's megacities should be fighting for policies that will help to neutralize the threat to the entire region, not just our own homes.

National governments will listen to us. After all, cities account for most of an economy's dynamism; without their catalytic force, Asia's rapid economic growth over the last four decades would not have been possible. And cities are the beating cultural heart of modern Asian societies.

It is time for Asia's urban leaders to use this influence, by banding together to help mitigate the threat posed by the rogue Kim regime. For starters, this means fighting to ensure that, unlike in the past, the United Nations sanctions imposed on North Korea are enforced to the letter.

At the same time, Asia's municipal leaders must use their own policing powers to prevent illicit wealth transfers from their jurisdictions to North Korea. This means pressuring financial institutions and, perhaps more important, unofficial money transfer networks, to halt any movement of funds to the North.

The leaders of Asia's major cities must also use every contact with Chinese officials to urge them to agitate for stronger efforts by President Xi Jinping's administration to rein in the Kim regime. Xi has so far been reluctant to tighten the screws on North Korea, owing largely to concerns about the potential consequences for China if the Kim regime collapses.

But the reality is that China's great urban centers now face the same threat from the Kim regime as their counterparts elsewhere in Asia. In fact, now that China has voiced support for UN sanctions – a step that probably left Kim feeling betrayed – China's cities may be among the most vulnerable.

Words are not enough; even the most heated rhetoric directed at the North has proved entirely useless, because it is not backed by action. For China, such action must reflect a full embrace of the goal of North Korean de-nuclearization. To that end, the key policy initiative that Japan, South Korea, and the United States must embrace is to negotiate, and conclude, an

2.

1:
PEDESTRIANS IN TOKYO WATCH THE
NEWS FOLLOWING A NORTH KOREAN
MISSILE TEST OVER JAPAN.

2:
RESIDENTS COVER THEIR HEADS
WHILE TAKING SHELTER DURING
AN EVACUATION DRILL IN JAPAN.

agreement with China about the security situation that will prevail on the Korean Peninsula should the Kim regime collapse.

The contours of such an agreement are not hard to discern. The US, Japan, and South Korea all hope for the eventual peaceful reunification of Korea. But China, fearing that outcome, needs assurances that America's military presence in South Korea, which has been shrinking for over two decades and no longer includes nuclear weapons, will not be extended northward, toward China's own border.

South Korea's government could offer those assurances, with the blessing of its Japanese and American allies, agreeing today in a formal treaty lodged at the UN that no foreign power's troops will be permitted to be stationed anywhere north of what is now the demilitarized zone that divides the two Koreas. Once the missile threat from the North was truly eliminated, South Korea could also remove the US-supplied Terminal High Altitude Area Defense (THAAD) missile system from its territory. As China has (wrongly) viewed the THAAD system as a threat to the viability of its own nuclear deterrent, such a move would eliminate what has become an open wound between the two countries.

To provide China with further assurances, and at no added risk to South Korea, Japan, or the US, the UN could also place peacekeeping forces and inspectors on the ground. A small number of Chinese soldiers and inspectors could even be included in these groups, so long as they take orders from UN appointed leaders.

This is the agenda for peace and security that Asia's cities, which have been leading the region into the future for decades now, should pursue in 2018. We must all now use our influence to ensure that ours is a future free from the threat of nuclear war. PS

Yuriko Koike, *Governor of Tokyo, has been Japan's defense minister, national security adviser, and a member of the National Diet.*

Xi Unbound?

MINXIN PEI
Professor, Claremont McKenna College

China has defied expectations yet again. President Xi Jinping, the chief of the Chinese Communist Party, was widely expected to face his toughest test so far in October, when the CCP convened its 19th National Congress to choose its next leadership. Though Xi was guaranteed a second five-year term, it was thought that he would run into serious opposition if he refused to appoint a successor. But he did just that – and the opposition never materialized.

The reason is simple: Xi was prepared. Since taking office in 2012, he has carried out a sustained crackdown on civil society, unleashing a wave of repression few thought would be possible in post-Mao China. He also pursued a large-scale anti-corruption campaign, which constrained and even eliminated potential political rivals, thereby enabling him to consolidate his power swiftly.

Early this year, when Chinese security agents abducted Xiao Jianhua, a China-born Hong Kong-based billionaire, to serve as a potential witness against senior leaders, any remaining resistance to Xi's push for greater authority was decimated. Nonetheless, to strengthen his position further in the run-up to the Congress, a sitting Politburo member who was viewed as a possible successor was abruptly arrested on corruption charges in July.

When the Congress finally arrived, Xi capitalized on this momentum to install two of his allies in the Politburo Standing Committee, the party's top decision-making body. And, by preventing the CCP from designating a successor, he has opened the door to a third term in 2022.

Judging by any conventional measure, Xi has thus emerged from 2017 more powerful than ever. The question now is whether he can use that power to translate his vision for China – particularly for its economy – into reality.

On this front, Xi made important progress in his first term, single-handedly corralling the Chinese bureaucracy to implement his ambitious but risky "Belt and Road Initiative" (BRI). That plan entails the use of Chinese financing, materials, and expertise to build infrastructure linking countries throughout Asia, Africa, and ➡

The new conventional wisdom is that Xi will be able to steamroll his colleagues in 2022, regardless of his performance in the coming five years.

Europe to the global economic juggernaut that China has become.

But, even with his significantly augmented power, Xi's continued success in implementing his economic vision is uncertain, at best, owing precisely to the ideological indoctrination and repression that underpin his authority. Despite the propaganda blitz lauding his vision for China, it is doubtful that many Chinese, including CCP members, really believe that their country's future lies in a centralized, fear-based authoritarian regime.

In fact, while overt resistance to Xi's vision is difficult to find – it is, after all, exceedingly dangerous nowadays – passive resistance is pervasive. And Xi's toughest opponents are not members of China's tiny dissident community, but rather the party bureaucrats who have borne the brunt of his anti-corruption drive, not just losing considerable illicit income and advantages, but also being subjected to unrelenting dread of politicized investigations.

Unless Xi can regain the support of the party's mid- and lower-level officials, his plan to remake China could fizzle out. After all, however powerful he might be, he cannot escape the reality captured by the ancient Chinese adage, "Mountains are high and the emperor is far away." And, without the promise of sufficient material reward, China's apparatchiks may subscribe to the logic that prevailed among citizens of the former Soviet bloc countries: "We pretend to work, and they pretend to pay us."

Beyond a recalcitrant bureaucracy, Xi might confront a serious challenge from the so-called Youth League faction of the CCP, affiliated with former President Hu Jintao. With two seats on the new seven-member Politburo Standing Committee being held by protégés of Hu, a power struggle between the Youth League and Xi's faction cannot be ruled out.

Of course, it is possible that Xi can overcome resistance from the Youth League. After all, he has already largely vanquished the faction connected to former President Jiang Zemin, which previously constituted the most powerful rival group within the CCP. But even if Xi subdues the Youth League, he will be left with a regime that is more fractured and dispirited.

Xi also faces significant policy challenges. On the economic front, he will have to contend with soaring debts and overcapacity, which, together with a shift toward protectionism in President Donald Trump's America, could depress growth further. In foreign policy, too, Xi will confront a deteriorating relationship with the United States, fueled by the intensifying North Korean nuclear threat and China's own aggressive behavior in the South China Sea.

The new conventional wisdom is that Xi will be able to steamroll his colleagues in 2022, regardless of his performance in the coming five years. This might be true. But political authority is ephemeral, especially for leaders who lack a solid economic track record. For now, Xi and his supporters have reason to celebrate. But they should not count on raising their glasses in five years. **PS**

Minxin Pei is Professor of Government at Claremont McKenna College and the author of China's Crony Capitalism.

2:
XI JINPING DELIVERS
A SPEECH AT THE
GREAT HALL OF THE
PEOPLE, BEIJING.

HEAD
SOUTH

BRAZILIANS
PROTESTING IN
RIO DE JANEIRO.

Latin America's *Annus Mediocris*

JORGE G. CASTAÑEDA
Former Secretary of Foreign Affairs of Mexico

The good, the bad, and "the Donald." For Latin America, that was 2017 in a nutshell.

The highlight of the year was, without question, the historic peace forged in Colombia. After a half-century-long insurgency fueled by drug cartels, Cubans, and money launderers, the Revolutionary Armed Forces of Colombia (FARC) laid down their weapons and entered the political mainstream. Although some Colombians felt that President Juan Manuel Santos gave away too much to reach the accord, the end of the Western Hemisphere's longest-running armed conflict should be lauded. Santos may not enjoy the domestic popularity his achievements merit, but the peace he championed – which earned him the Nobel Peace Prize in 2016 – is likely to survive.

Another highlight of the last 12 months was Latin America's continued success in tackling corruption, led by Brazil's *Lava Jato* (Car Wash) investigation. That probe, which began in 2014, netted a number of high-profile politicians and business leaders in 2017, including former Presidents Dilma Rousseff and Luiz Inácio "Lula" da Silva in Brazil; three former presidents of Peru; and a former head of Mexico's state oil company, Pemex. Santos also had to testify – and deny that he was aware of contributions to his campaigns from the Brazilian construction conglomerate Odebrecht.

Corruption charges were also lodged during the year against Venezuelan President Nicolás Maduro, Guatemalan President Jimmy Morales, several former Mexican state governors, and former Argentine President Cristina Fernández de Kirchner, along with a handful of those who served in her cabinet. ➔

The sheer volume of corruption cases is staggering, and some worry that the region's political stability could suffer as a result. In Brazil, for example, many fear the judiciary's tenacity could lead to a military dictatorship or the equivalent, especially if an extreme right-wing former soldier is elected president next year.

These are not groundless concerns, given the region's history of authoritarianism. But with endemic corruption eroding Latin America's economic growth and undermining the rule of law, the investigations underway are a welcome change from the *status quo*.

Latin America's low point in 2017 was, like its highs, easy to discern: Venezuela's political crisis. Protests that erupted in the middle of the year and lasted through September resulted in the deaths of more than 120 anti-government demonstrators. Many were killed at the hands of barely disguised pro-government Chavistas, known as *colectivos*.

On balance, Trump's arrival on the world stage made 2017 a year to forget for Latin America.

In July, Maduro replaced the elected National Assembly with a handpicked constituent assembly to rewrite the constitution and entrench his regime. The crisis, fueled by the government's massive foreign-debt burden, effectively shut down government services, and basic necessities like food, medicines, and toilet paper remain scarce. Some two million Venezuelans have fled the country.

Most Latin American governments have refused to recognize Maduro's *de facto coup d'état* – an encouraging example of democratic solidarity in the region. But Maduro has yet to engage in good-faith negotiations, and Latin America's worst crisis seems no closer to resolution.

Finally, there was US President Donald Trump's effect on Latin America in 2017. While the impact of Trump's presidency has been felt around the world, no region has suffered as profoundly as those on the United States' southern doorstep.

Consider the crisis in Venezuela, which was moving toward resolution before Trump suggested that a military response might be needed. As Venezuela's defense minister put it, Trump's reckless comments were "an act of craziness" – one that forced several Latin American leaders to distance themselves from the US. By refusing to rule out a military option, Trump effectively torpedoed any chance of a speedy resolution, allowing Maduro to portray the incident as proof that "*el imperio*" wanted to overthrow him.

Trump's policies and statements on immigration were equally chilling, especially for Mexico, Cuba, and the countries of Central America, which account for a majority of immigrants in the US. From vowing to end a program shielding young undocumented immigrants from deportation, to his absurd pledge to build a "wall" on the border with Mexico, Trump's behavior has been deeply unsettling.

Beyond immigration, Cuba and Mexico were in Trump's crosshairs, for different reasons.

On Cuba, Trump rolled back much of President Barack Obama's efforts to normalize bilateral relations. The new US policies, implemented mid-year, were not draconian, but they probably will suffice to dissuade new American investment. Trump's decision to reduce the number of staff at the US Embassy

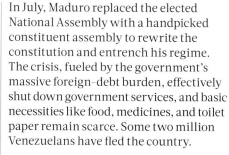

1.

in Havana, officially due to a mysterious illness affecting them, has only heightened investor concerns. And, as the State Department continues to discourage Americans from visiting Cuba by issuing ominous travel advisories, the number of US tourists is likely to decline in 2018.

As for Mexico, Trump's insistence on renegotiating the North American Free Trade Agreement battered the peso, discouraged foreign investment, and put the country's highly unpopular president, Enrique Peña Nieto, in a predicament. Following negotiations in Mexico, Canada, and the US in 2017, it became increasingly evident that Trump's strident campaign rhetoric was being translated into policy, most of which is unacceptable to America's trading partners.

The year that just ended was an eventful one for Latin America. A war ended, dense webs of high-level corruption began to unravel, and the risk of authoritarian backsliding in some countries has underscored the region's broader commitment to democracy.

But, on balance, Trump's arrival on the world stage made 2017 a year to forget for Latin America. Millions of Latinos in the US have been targeted for deportation, and countless others will suffer in Mexico,

Cuba, and elsewhere if the US proceeds with the administration's proposed trade and immigration policies. And that, unfortunately, is the most likely scenario for 2018 and beyond. PS

Jorge G. Castañeda, *Mexico's Secretary of Foreign Affairs from 2000–2003, is Global Distinguished Professor of Politics and Latin American and Caribbean Studies at New York University.*

1:
PEOPLE SUNBATHE ON A HOTEL ROOFTOP AS PROTESTERS MARCH ALONG COPACABANA BEACH.

2:
THE US-MEXICAN BORDER FENCE AT PLAYAS DE TIJUANA, MEXICO.

VENEZUELA'S STRUGGLE FOR FREEDOM

MARÍA CORINA MACHADO
Former Member of the
Venezuelan National Assembly

1:
AN ACTIVIST THROWS TEAR GAS BACK AT
THE POLICE DURING A PROTEST AGAINST
PRESIDENT NICOLÁS MADURO.

2:
MARÍA CORINA MACHADO.

3:
NICOLÁS MADURO.

4:
CUBAN PRESIDENT RAÚL CASTRO.

The wave of violent protests that swept Venezuela this year focused global attention on my country's plight. Millions of Venezuelans left the country, and many more are trying to flee from hunger, disease, and oppression. President Nicolás Maduro, rather than seeking to end the suffering, has taken steps to entrench his dictatorial rule, drawing worldwide condemnation.

But while Venezuela's crisis is now firmly on the international community's radar, few have fully grasped why it is happening, or what a slide into autocracy might mean beyond the country's borders. A regime that has transformed a once-prosperous country into a basket case of poverty and crime is a threat not only to Venezuelans, but also to decades of democratic progress in the region.

Maduro's despotism has been compared to Raúl Castro's hold on Cuba. But, rather than a full-blown totalitarian regime, what we have in Venezuela is, to borrow a term from the German legal theorist Carl Schmitt, a permanent "state of exception." Using the illusion of free elections as a smokescreen, Maduro has sought to strip Venezuela's democracy of its substance by subordinating all key institutions, especially the National Electoral Council, to the government.

Amid this democratic ruse, the regime kills, tortures, persecutes, and exiles opponents, threatens and intimidates critics, and censors or closes down media outlets, slowly asphyxiating freedom. In relying on piecemeal subjugation, the regime seems intent on not crossing some invisible "red line" that might force the international community to take a tougher stand.

Sadly, at the moment, Maduro need not worry. With the Cold War a distant memory, the West's threat-perception mechanisms have weakened. Many Western leaders struggle to grasp the dangers that Maduro's regime poses to the stability of Latin American democracies, to the West's security in general, and to the national interests of the United States

in particular. Aside from US President Donald Trump's refusal to rule out a military option, most global commitments to Venezuela's pro-democracy efforts have been anemic.

There are numerous reasons why stronger international pressure is needed. For starters, Maduro's regime continues to supply Cuba with Venezuelan oil and money to shore up Castro's dictatorship. No prudent observer could welcome the long-term implications of this partnership.

The Maduro regime also supports, and often finances, a host of destabilizing political forces, from radical parties and secessionist groups in Spain, the United Kingdom, and across Europe, to well-known terrorist organizations in the Middle East, where it cultivates strong connections with Iran and radical Islamists (continuing the policies of its predecessor). Moreover, Venezuela's government often supports anti-Western diplomatic initiatives at the United Nations, and stirs up division and strife within regional bodies, like the Organization of American States.

And lest we forget, the regime's ties to Colombian and Mexican drug cartels, money launderers, and arms traffickers are all well documented.

During the confrontations with the regime that took place throughout Venezuela this year, unarmed, courageous, and determined people directly challenged Maduro's security forces, demonstrating that Venezuelans will resist attacks on their freedom. The sacrifices people – especially the young – have already made bear witness to this commitment.

So, what happens next? Regime change, a top priority for many, can still be accomplished, but only with the right tools. To topple the forces of illiberalism and challenge the ruling clique, Venezuelans will need a solid strategy of civil disobedience. This will require continued external pressure on the government's financial and institutional sources of support, and sustained mobilization of domestic protest.

This is not a strategy that the entire opposition movement advocates. Some believe that pro-democracy forces have been defeated by dictatorship, and that the only way to challenge this new normal is by seeking to ameliorate it from within.

But such an approach will lead only to appeasement, cohabitation, and eventual submission.

History suggests that when a country is pushed to the edge, its patriots fight back. For that reason, I believe that, in the coming months, a reinvigorated opposition will once again shake the country. As people come to recognize that Maduro's regime has no interest in mitigating the social and economic catastrophe that has befallen Venezuela, protests will reignite.

Today, Venezuela lies in wait. Pro-democracy political parties and civil-society groups are reorganizing, sowing the seeds of a new and more powerful push for freedom. Together with international partners, Venezuelan democrats will continue to work to fracture the regime and reclaim our freedom.

Venezuelans owe a debt of gratitude to those in the international community who have already answered our pleas. Now, as 2017 comes to an end, we once more ask our friends abroad to cease all ambiguity and stop calling for a dialogue with a regime that has shown no interest in negotiating. Instead, we ask world leaders to support the legitimate National Assembly, and to recognize the Supreme Court, which was forced into exile. And all free countries should continue exposing the "narco-dictatorship" that currently governs.

Venezuela stands at a crossroads. In one direction lies appeasement of the consolidation of criminal rule – a path that implies incalculable costs for the region and the world. In the other direction lies regime change, restoration of democratic institutions, the end of the humanitarian crisis, and the renewed promise of economic and political prosperity.

We Venezuelans must decide which path we will take. But we need the support of the global community if we are to make the right choice. **PS**

María Corina Machado is a former member of the National Assembly of Venezuela, and the founder of Súmante, a Caracas-based election-monitoring organization.

Revolutionary Centrism

TONY BLAIR
Former British Prime Minister

T he center ground of Western politics is known as the field of pragmatism, quiet reason, and evolution, where political actors eschew extremes and seek compromise. Because political centrists are distrustful of loud-mouthed and divisive rhetoric, they have taken a somewhat *de haut en bas* view of the way the political world functions.

First, we must understand the need for radical change, not merely incremental reforms.

Now they are being overwhelmed. Populism of the right and the left is rampant. The old rules no longer apply. Things said which would have disqualified a candidate a few years back are now a passport to voters' hearts. Policy positions previously regarded as mainstream are sneered at, and those regarded as outlandish are very much inland today. And political alliances that have endured for a century or more are breaking apart, owing to profound social, economic, and cultural changes.

The right is fissuring. The prevailing sentiment is nationalist, anti-immigration, and often protectionist, giving rise to a new alliance. In the United Kingdom, traditional Labour supporters in old industrial communities and wealthy de-regulators and business owners have united in their dislike of the way the world is changing and "political correctness." Whether this coalition – and similar formations in other countries – can survive its inherent economic contradictions is unclear, though I would not underestimate the cohesive power of a shared sense of cultural alienation.

But, as can be seen in the fighting within the Republican Party in the United States, the Conservative Party in Britain, and across Europe, a significant part of the right still sees itself as championing free trade, open markets, and immigration as a positive force.

The left is also dividing. One part is moving to a much more traditional statist position on economic policy, and to a form of identity politics that is much more radical on cultural norms. The other part clings to an attempt to provide a unifying national narrative around concepts of social justice and economic progress.

Of course, what used to be called the mainstream of both the left and the right could take back control of their political parties. For now, however, the extremes are in charge, leaving many – socially liberal and in favor of a competitive market economy alongside modern forms of collective action – without a political home.

Is this temporary, or are we at an inflection point?

It is globalization that is changing politics. The real division today is between those who view globalization essentially as an opportunity carrying risks that should be mitigated; and those who believe that, despite its apparent advantages, globalization is destroying our way of life and should be heavily constrained.

I have sometimes expressed this as the difference between an "open" and "closed" view of the world. But while that language captures some of the essence of the difference, I have come to think it is inadequate, because it doesn't pay sufficient respect to the feeling that the "globalizers" are ignoring genuine problems with the way their creation is working.

The danger of Western politics is that, without a broad and stable center ground, the two extremes meet in uncompromising confrontation. The degree of polarization in both the US and the UK is frightening. In both cases, the public is dividing itself into two nations that don't think like each other, work with each other, or actually like each other.

This is dangerous, because if it persists, democracy loses its appeal. Government becomes paralyzed. The strongman model becomes more attractive. When our political and economic systems become a competition animated by a winner-take-

all mentality, those who win at some point begin to regard the losers as enemies, rather than opponents.

Democracy has a spirit, not just a form; and today's level of polarization is inconsistent with it. That is why we need a new politics that seeks to build bridges and bring people together – a politics that differs from the centrist politics of yesterday in two respects.

First, we must understand the need for radical change, not merely incremental reforms. Technology alone will transform the way we live, work, and think. We must show those feeling left behind that there is a way through the challenge of change and that it is transformative. And we should address their understandable anxieties over issues like immigration, which are complex and multilayered, and cannot simply be dismissed as whining by nativist "deplorables."

In other words, we must show that we have listened to the legitimate sense of grievance about certain aspects of globalization.

Second, we have to acknowledge that contemporary politics is not operating adequately to meet the challenge. While it remains taboo for politicians occupying the center ground in traditional parties to work with each other, they are ineffective, unable to say what they really believe, and unable to represent those who urgently need to be represented.

In short, in these times, revolution is too much the zeitgeist to be left to the extremes. The center should also become capable of exploding the *status quo*. PS

Tony Blair, Prime Minister of the United Kingdom from 1997 to 2007, is Chairman of the Africa Governance Initiative.

STEALING THE POPULISTS' CLOTHES

RADOSŁAW SIKORSKI
Former Polish Foreign Minister

Two cheers for US President Donald Trump. Without him, the West would still regard populism as a problem unique to Central and Eastern Europe. Yet Trump's presidency is as clear a demonstration as there could be of the fact that populism is not merely a product of the alleged "immaturity" of post-communist countries. ➡

SEBASTIAN KURZ, LEADER OF THE
AUSTRIAN PEOPLE'S PARTY, SPEAKS
TO SUPPORTERS AFTER WINNING
THE PARLIAMENTARY ELECTION
ON OCTOBER 15, 2017.

Leo Tolstoy supposedly said that the further one is from events, the more inevitable those events seem. So it is with today's populist surge. It wasn't inevitable that Poland's Law and Justice Party (PiS) would come to power with 38% of the vote in 2015; nor was it inevitable that Trump would win the US presidency, despite having received almost three million fewer votes than his opponent. In both cases, luck and the competition's incompetence played a role, just as they did in bringing decidedly liberal forces to power in France in 2017.

Still, as we head into 2018, we should recognize that another year of populist turbulence beckons. After all, there is nothing new about populist politics in democracies, whether young or old. In the nineteenth century, the "free silver" movement divided the United States in much the same way that Brexit divides Britain today.

Populists succeed by exploiting citizens' alienation from an establishment that has failed or is unable to respond to some salient challenge – for example, low crop prices and debt deflation in the US in the 1870s, or migration in the European Union today. They usually propose simple solutions to complex problems. And once in power, they usually fail to deliver on their promises, but only after they have spent all the public's money. Wise establishmentarians accommodate some populist arguments within their own political programs. After these concessions are made, emotions tend to cool, and social stability can be restored.

So, what are the foremost populist grievances today? Judging by countries like Poland and Hungary, there are at least three: class resentment, demographic despair, and threatened identities. Each of these grievances has a legitimate basis, and all need to be addressed.

Contrary to popular belief, none of these grievances is strictly economic. In Poland, incomes have been rising and inequalities have been falling for 25 years. Yet at the same time, ordinary people have become increasingly suspicious of elites "feeding at the trough" while everyone else allegedly struggles to make ends meet.

Part of the problem is that expectations have outrun reality. When expectations go unmet, people begin to suspect that the social compact itself is unfair. It is this sense of unfairness, far more than income levels, that has fueled support for populist movements. After all, one can earn much more than the Polish minimum wage and still resent the fact that the global rich are squirreling away trillions of dollars in tax havens, or that transnational companies routinely shirk their tax obligations.

Moreover, populists, despite their racist rhetoric on the issue of migration, are not wrong to intuit that a generous welfare state is incompatible with open borders. There are a billion people on the other side of the Mediterranean Sea who cannot be blamed for wanting to live in a European welfare state. Many of them live in countries with neither welfare nor even a functioning state.

Europe cannot accept everyone. There are legitimate discussions to be had about tolerable immigration rates, Western countries' absorptive capacity, and border controls. Moreover, it is fair to ask if there are better ways than mass migration to address the problems associated with an aging population, such as by extending child benefits and parental leave. What has been most irksome to populists and their sympathizers is that merely raising such questions exposes one to accusations of intolerance, or worse.

As to the third populist grievance, it was predictable that those left behind in the age of globalization and meritocracy would fall back on collective identities as a source of dignity. And in Poland and the US, in particular, this trend has been reinforced by a decline in religiosity. Nationalism is the last refuge of those who fear losing a way of life. It is partly a reaction of endangered majorities that do not want to become minorities.

Now, alongside this list of grievances, consider the fact that, historically, every communications revolution has led to a political revolution. In a world of unregulated social media, populist demagogues do not have to do much to stoke the confusion, paranoia, and cynicism that are already smoldering within the electorate.

Looking forward, policymakers and political leaders need to address the fundamental concerns that populists have tapped. First, we need to fix capitalism, by ensuring that social contributions

1.

2.

> ## "Like any world-changing invention, digital technologies have obvious downsides that cannot be ignored."

are rewarded more appropriately than they are today. Even if we concede that financiers make a larger social contribution than doctors, are we really expected to believe that they contribute a thousand – let alone ten thousand – times more?

Likewise, it is time to freeze out companies and individuals that maintain accounts in OECD-designated tax havens. The EU, for its part, is right to insist that multinationals pay taxes wherever they do business. Member states need to support the Commission's proposals for tougher controls.

Second, governments need to reassert control over national – or, in the case of the EU, supranational – borders. Citizens want a say over who comes to live in their midst, and under what conditions. And they want to ensure that those who do come plan to be good neighbors.

Third, politicians must stop mining cheap nationalism for tactical electoral advantages. They owe it to voters to explain why their interests will be better protected through multilateralism. This is especially true for the EU, which needs to cultivate more European patriotism, perhaps through joint military action on the periphery.

Finally, the Internet, social media, and other new technologies need to be regulated, either by pressuring companies to police themselves, or by enacting new legislation. Like any world-changing invention, digital technologies have obvious downsides that cannot be ignored.

These are difficult but achievable goals. Contrary to the defeatism that has become rampant nowadays, we can, through democratic means, enact legislation and adopt regulations that address the problems populists have identified. But we need to hurry. If we don't act, the populists will – and with far more damaging results. **PS**

1:
THOUSANDS OF NATIONALISTS
AND FAR-RIGHT MEMBERS
MARCHING IN WARSAW.

2:
REFUGEES LEARN ABOUT GERMANY'S
DEMOCRATIC POLITICAL SYSTEM
AT A SHELTER FOR MIGRANTS.

*Radosław Sikorski is a former
Polish foreign minister.*

The Venal Roots of Political Turmoil

JANINE R. WEDEL

Professor, George Mason University

In 2017, corruption became a byword for politics on almost every continent, framing government action in countries as different as China, Saudi Arabia, and Brazil. Corruption and its attendant scandals toppled presidents and prime ministers, cut down political opposition leaders, and fueled "populist" revolts worldwide. Without accounting for systemic official misconduct, our current era of political turbulence simply doesn't make sense.

In Brazil, investigations have been ongoing into what one judge has described as a "scheme of systemic corruption" between public officials and the Brazilian oil giant Petrobras. As a result of the investigations, President Dilma Rousseff was impeached and removed from office in August 2016, and former President Luiz Inácio "Lula" da Silva was convicted and sentenced to prison in July of this year.

Similarly, in South Korea, a corruption scandal led to President Park Geun-hye's impeachment and removal from office in March, and to the imprisonment of Lee Jae-yong, the heir apparent at Samsung, in August.

In Pakistan, Prime Minister Nawaz Sharif was ousted by the country's Supreme Court in July. He is now facing corruption charges for London real-estate purchases that he allegedly made in the 1990s through offshore companies and under his children's names. The assets had gone unreported until they were revealed by the 2015 leak of the "Panama Papers."

In Russia under President Vladimir Putin, corruption flourishes at the nexus of state politics and big business, with loyal oligarchs also reliably executing Putin's political agendas. But corruption is also being exported. Indeed, Putin spreads his formula of illiberalism, nationalism, and authoritarianism to former Soviet states, Europe, and even the US.

And in Hungary, allegations of cronyism have dogged Prime Minister Viktor Orbán, who has strengthened his hold on power by cultivating close ties with the country's oligarchs.

As I have documented over the past decade, corruption is not just about graft or illicit transactions. It also includes legal violations of the public trust, often committed by "shadow elites" who assume a tangle of roles in the public and private sectors, sometimes simultaneously. ➔

1:
RUSSIAN OPPOSITION LEADER
ALEXEI NAVALNY LEAVES A
POLICE STATION IN MOSCOW.

1.

1:
BRAZIL'S FORMER PRESIDENTS
LUIZ INÁCIO "LULA" DA SILVA
AND DILMA ROUSSEFF.

Trump himself has imbued public corruption with a level of flamboyancy unlike anything America has seen in decades – if ever.

The proliferation of officials pursuing their own interests and escaping accountability has not been lost on ordinary people. In the US, what I call the "new corruption" was a central concern of both the Tea Party on the right and Occupy Wall Street on the left. Both movements objected to the 2008 Wall Street bailout, and saw it as evidence of a rigged system.

In each of the last three years, Chapman University's "Survey of American Fears" found that concerns about corruption weigh more heavily on Americans' minds than even crime, terrorism, or deaths in the family. Donald Trump won the presidency in 2016 partly by exploiting these concerns. Yet despite his promise to "drain the swamp," he spent 2017 expanding and deepening it. All manner of Trump associates have found work and increased their cachet on K-street, Washington's lobbying hub. Some have sought work lobbying for foreign powers, even though candidate Trump railed against his rival for supposed foreign influence. Moreover, Trump assembled a team of advisers with direct financial connections to the sectors they are supposed to oversee, as well as former lobbyists, including some working for foreign regimes. Trump himself has imbued public corruption with a level of flamboyancy unlike anything America has seen in decades – if ever.

Among his many violations of the public trust, Trump has declined to fully divest from his business holdings or release his tax returns and has installed family members in powerful official and unofficial positions.

Moreover, some of Trump's cabinet members have tapped into public resources for their own personal and private use. So far, the only official to have been held accountable for this is Tom Price, who resigned as Secretary of Health and Human Services in September, after news outlets reported that he had billed taxpayers for numerous chartered flights.

Trump and his associates might very well face serious corruption charges eventually, depending on what former FBI Director Robert Mueller finds in his ever-widening investigation into Russian interference in the 2016 election. Already, Mueller has brought charges against Trump's former campaign chairman, Paul Manafort, and Manafort's longtime associate, Rick Gates. Many observers doubt that the Trump administration will last until the end of its electoral term in 2020.

But citizens should be forewarned that when anti-corruption efforts ensnare senior officials, a lengthy period of uncertainty often follows. For example, the vast anti-corruption investigation in Brazil has won international praise, but it has not restored political or financial stability. On the contrary, according to the Council on Foreign Relations, Brazil is suffering "unprecedented voter dissatisfaction," with no obvious leader to rebuild public trust.

What follows from anti-corruption investigations depends largely on a country's political and economic context. For example, because political power in Pakistan is routinely shuffled among family members, Sharif, upon being deposed, tried to name his brother as his successor. In September, his wife was elected to fill his former parliamentary seat.

In other countries, anti-corruption probes have been used by authoritarian regimes to neutralize opponents. In July, Poland's government, controlled by the illiberal Law and Justice (PiS) party, partly succeeded in its efforts to subordinate the judiciary to political control, arguing that the courts had been corrupted by "elites."

And in China, President Xi Jinping has made savvy use of an anti-corruption campaign to purge political rivals and settle scores – a campaign that Saudi Arabia's Crown Prince Mohammed bin Salman appears to be mimicking

in his effort to concentrate power in his own hands. Owing to its one-party system, China has been able to keep up the appearance of stability during its intensifying crackdown. But some analysts argue that widespread discontent is brewing beneath the surface, and that endemic corruption among the country's ruling elites is eroding the political system's sustainability.

That points to a final visible trend this year: citizens pushing back against corruption in all of its forms. In Poland, widespread protests forced the president to veto much of the PiS's attempted judicial power grab. In Venezuela, protests against cronyism were ongoing throughout the year. And in Russia, thousands of citizens took to the streets to protest Putin's kleptocratic regime – inspired, in part, by the anti-corruption activist Alexei Navalny, who has been mobilizing the Russian opposition with his "crooks and thieves" campaign targeting Putin's United Russia party.

In many countries nowadays, civic activism may be absent on most issues. But corruption isn't one of them. People cared enough about it to upend politics in 2016 and again in 2017. There is no reason to believe that 2018 will be any different. **PS**

Janine R. Wedel, an anthropologist and University Professor at the Schar School of Policy and Government at George Mason University, is the author of UNACCOUNTABLE: How the Establishment Corrupted Our Finances, Freedom, and Politics and Created an Outsider Class.

Making Social Media Safe for Democracy

**SAMANTHA BRADSHAW
& PHILIP N. HOWARD**
Oxford Internet Institute

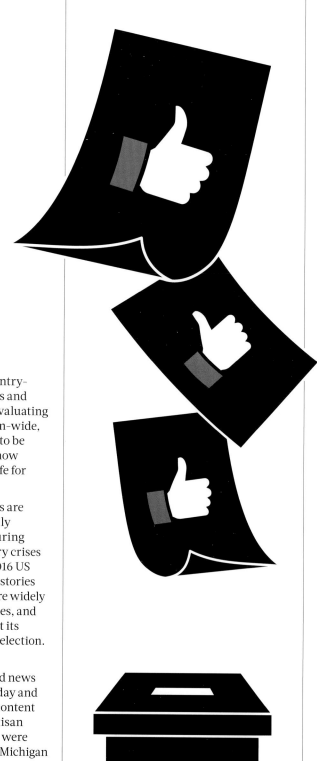

In the run-up to multiple votes around the world in 2016, including the United Kingdom's Brexit vote and the United States presidential election, social media companies like Facebook and Twitter systematically served large numbers of voters poor-quality information – indeed, often outright lies – about politics and public policy. Though those companies have been widely criticized, the junk news – sensational stories, conspiracy theories, and other disinformation – flowed on through 2017.

While a growing number of country-specific fact-checking initiatives and some interesting new apps for evaluating junk news have emerged, system-wide, technical solutions do not seem to be on offer from the platforms. So how should we make social media safe for democratic norms?

We know that social media firms are serving up vast amounts of highly polarizing content to citizens during referenda, elections, and military crises around the world. During the 2016 US presidential election, fake news stories were shared on social media more widely than professionally produced ones, and the distribution of junk news hit its highest point the day before the election.

Other types of highly polarizing content from Kremlin-controlled news organizations such as Russia Today and Sputnik, as well as repurposed content from WikiLeaks and hyper-partisan commentary packaged as news, were concentrated in swing states like Michigan and Pennsylvania. Similar patterns occurred in France during the presidential election in April and May, in the UK during the general election in June, and in Germany throughout 2017 as the federal election in September approached.

Around the world, the coordinated effort to use social media as a conduit for junk news has fueled cynicism, increased divisions between citizens and parties, and influenced the broader media agenda. The "success" of these efforts is reflected in the sheer speed with which they have spread.

As any epidemiologist knows, the first step toward controlling a communicable disease is to understand how it is transmitted. Junk news is distributed through automation and the proprietary black box algorithms that determine what is and is not relevant news and information. We call this "computational propaganda," because it involves politically motivated lies backed by the global reach and power of social media platforms like Facebook, Google, and Twitter.

Throughout the recent elections in the Western democracies, social media firms actively chased ad revenue from political campaigns and distributed content without considering its veracity. Indeed, Facebook, Google, and Twitter had staff embedded at Trump's digital campaign headquarters in San Antonio. Foreign governments and marketing firms in Eastern Europe operated fake Facebook, Google, and Twitter accounts, and spent hundreds of thousands of dollars on political advertisements that targeted voters with divisive messages.

To understand the how pervasive these problems are, we took an in-depth look at computational propaganda in nine countries – Brazil, Canada, China, Germany, Poland, Russia, Taiwan, Ukraine, and the United States – and a comparative look at 28 others. We have also analyzed the spread of computational propaganda during specific referenda and elections during the last year (and in the past, we have studied Mexico and Venezuela). Globally, the evidence doesn't bode well for democratic institutions.

One crucial finding is that social media platforms play a significant role in political engagement. Indeed, they are the primary vehicle by which young people develop their political identities. In the world's democracies, the majority of voters use social media to share political news and information, especially during elections. In countries where only small proportions of the public have regular access to social media, such platforms are still fundamental infrastructure for

political conversation among journalists, civil-society leaders, and political elites.

Moreover, social media platforms are actively used to manipulate public opinion, though in diverse ways and on different topics. In authoritarian countries, social media platforms are one of the primary means of preventing popular unrest, especially true during political and security crises.

Ultimately, designing for democracy, in systematic ways, would vindicate the original promise of social media.

Almost half of the political conversation over Russian Twitter, for example, is mediated by highly automated accounts. The biggest collections of fake accounts are managed by marketing firms in Poland and Ukraine.

Among democracies, we find that social media platforms are actively used for computational propaganda, either through broad efforts at opinion manipulation or targeted experiments on particular segments of the public. In Brazil, bots had a significant role in shaping public debate ahead of the election of former President Dilma Rousseff, during her impeachment in early 2017, and amid the country's ongoing constitutional crisis. In every country, we found civil-society groups struggling to protect themselves and respond to active misinformation campaigns.

Facebook says that it will work to combat these information operations, and it has taken some positive steps. It has started to examine how foreign governments use its platform to manipulate voters in democracies. Before the French presidential election last spring, it removed some 30,000 fake accounts. It purged thousands more ahead of the British election in June,

and then tens of thousands before the German election in September.

But firms like Facebook now need to engineer a more fundamental shift from defensive and reactive platform tweaks to more proactive and imaginative ways of supporting democratic cultures. With more critical political moments coming in 2018 – Egypt, Brazil, and Mexico will all hold general elections, and strategists in the US are already planning for the midterm congressional election in November – such action is urgent.

Let's assume that authoritarian governments will continue to view social media as a tool for political control. But we should also assume that encouraging civic engagement, fostering electoral participation, and promoting news and information from reputable outlets are crucial to democracy. Ultimately, designing for democracy, in systematic ways, would vindicate the original promise of social media.

Unfortunately, social media companies tend to blame their own user communities for what has gone wrong. Facebook still declines to collaborate with researchers seeking to understand the impact of social media on democracy, and to defer responsibility for fact-checking the content it disseminates.

Social media firms may not be creating this nasty content, but they provide the platforms that have allowed computational propaganda to become one of the most powerful tools currently being used to undermine democracy. If democracy is to survive, today's social media giants will have to redesign themselves. 18

Samantha Bradshaw *is a researcher on the Computational Propaganda Project at the University of Oxford.*

Philip N. Howard *is Professor of Sociology and Director of the Oxford Internet Institute at the University of Oxford.*

Subscribe Now

Exclusive explainers, thematic deep dives, interviews with world leaders, and more. Choose an *On Point* subscription that's right for you.

All Access

UNLIMITED ACCESS
& FREE SHIPPING

Print & Digital Subscription
Long Reads; Insider Interviews; Global Bookmarks; and our printed magazine, The Year Ahead

- Annual subscription
- Our printed magazine, *The Year Ahead*
- Unlimited access to *On Point*, including:
  · Longer, in-depth commentaries
  · Book reviews
  · Exclusive interviews
  · All the commentaries in our *Year Ahead* magazine
- Unlimited access to our archive

$65 PER YEAR

Premium Access

UNLIMITED ACCESS

Digital Subscription
Long Reads; Insider Interviews; Global Bookmarks

- Annual subscription
- Unlimited access to *On Point*, including:
  · Longer, in-depth commentaries
  · Book reviews
  · Exclusive interviews
  · All the commentaries in our *Year Ahead* magazine
- Unlimited access to our archive

$50 PER YEAR

Print Subscription

FREE SHIPPING

Print Subscription
Our printed magazine, The Year Ahead

- Annual subscription
- Our printed magazine, *The Year Ahead*
  · Featuring commentaries looking back on the year that was and looking ahead to the year to come
- Unlimited access to our archive

$20 PER YEAR

Education and corporate subscription options are also available at discounted prices. Contact us at subscriptions@project-syndicate.org for more details.

project-syndicate.org/subscribe

The Carbon Policy Footprint
Corporate impact on climate policy may be more important than physical emissions...

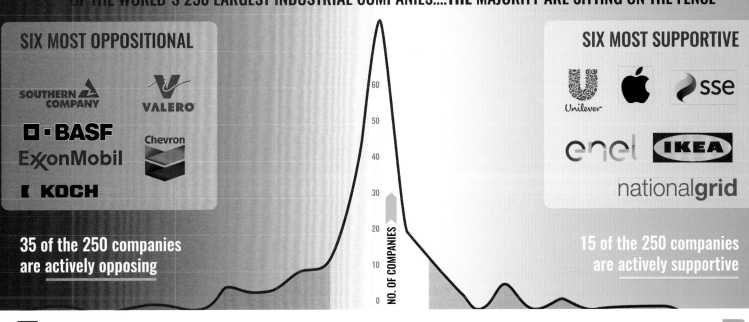

OF THE WORLD'S 250 LARGEST INDUSTRIAL COMPANIES....THE MAJORITY ARE SITTING ON THE FENCE

SIX MOST OPPOSITIONAL

SOUTHERN COMPANY   VALERO

BASF   Chevron

ExxonMobil

KOCH

35 of the 250 companies are actively opposing

SIX MOST SUPPORTIVE

Unilever   Apple   sse

enel   IKEA

national**grid**

15 of the 250 companies are actively supportive

NO. OF COMPANIES

60 / 50 / 40 / 30 / 20 / 10 / 0

◀ **INCREASING OPPOSITION**   **NEUTRAL**   **INCREASING SUPPORT** ▶

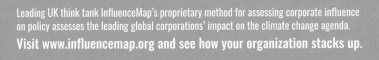

Leading UK think tank InfluenceMap's proprietary method for assessing corporate influence on policy assesses the leading global corporations' impact on the climate change agenda.
Visit www.influencemap.org and see how your organization stacks up.

IM InfluenceMap

49

GLOBAL
WARNING

Donald Trump's election seemed to sound the death knell in the effort to roll back climate change. Instead, as Laurence Tubiana, Edmund S. Phelps, and the heads of the world's nine development banks point out in the essays that follow, Trump has been a catalyst for the profound shift in mindset needed to address the existential threat the world currently faces. Together, their contributions show that overcoming that threat is increasingly being seen as an opportunity, and that the transition to a green economy will continue to be a major source of innovation and economic dynamism.

A Year of Renewed Climate Commitments

LAURENCE TUBIANA
*CEO of the European
Climate Foundation*

For the growing share of the world's population that understands the existential threat posed by climate change, the beginning of 2017 brought a sense of trepidation. In fact, collective angst was already apparent at the 2016 United Nations Climate Change Conference in Marrakech, Morocco, which had just started when Donald Trump was elected president of the United States.

At that time, speculation was swirling about what Trump's election would mean for the US and the world. But there was little doubt that it would be bad for America's formal commitment to reduce greenhouse-gas emissions and mitigate the worst effects of climate change.

Throughout the course of 2017, questions about what a Trump presidency would entail began to be answered. And it turned out that while Trump certainly holds the most powerful office in the world when it comes to ordering military strikes, his power to refute the scientific consensus regarding climate change, and to resist the global transition to a green economy, is rather limited.

In Marrakech, the obstacles that Trump would confront were already apparent. Trump's criticisms of the 2015 Paris climate agreement were widely rejected, and all countries in attendance reiterated their commitment to the accord. They promised to continue reducing greenhouse-gas emissions, regardless of whether Trump followed through on his campaign's vow to "cancel Paris."

Of course, the question of whether Trump would actually keep this campaign promise ended up consuming the first several months of 2017, with a veritable soap opera – or rather, a domestic farce – playing out in the White House. Trump's daughter Ivanka and her husband, Jared Kushner, reportedly supported the Paris accord. But Scott Pruitt, the administrator of the Environmental Protection Agency, and his fellow climate-change deniers convinced Trump to withdraw the US from the agreement.

When that announcement finally came, on June 1, it was certainly disappointing. But it also gave new momentum to the task at hand. Within hours, Washington state Governor Jay Inslee declared: "We heard the president wanted to run up the white flag of surrender. We wanted to send a strong message to the world: We're not going to surrender." And in response to Trump's claim that he was "elected to represent the citizens of Pittsburgh, not Paris," Pittsburgh Mayor Bill Peduto announced that the "Steel City" would be shifting to 100% renewable-energy sources by 2035.

Peduto's vocal rebuke of Trump opened a window onto a quiet revolution that has been taking place across the US. He, along with 382 other US mayors, is a member of the Climate Mayors coalition, which represents 68 million Americans. Similarly, 14 US states and the hurricane-ravaged territory of Puerto Rico have banded together to form the United States Climate Alliance. All of these cities and states are committed to implementing the Barack Obama-era Clean Power Plan, despite Pruitt's efforts to abolish it. Similarly, more than 1,000 US

Trump or no Trump, the shift to renewable energies is irreversible.

companies have vowed to meet America's commitments under the Paris agreement.

This trend is not limited to the US. President Xi Jinping of China, the world's largest producer of greenhouse-gas pollution, also has reaffirmed his country's commitment to the Paris accord, and is encouraging all other signatories to do the same. At the Communist Party of China's 19th National Congress in October, he reiterated that China is in the "driver's seat" of international cooperation on climate change.

And in July 2017, all of the G20 governments, with the exception of the US, signed a statement emphasizing the importance and irreversibility of the Paris agreement.

This declaration echoed an earlier joint statement from the German, Italian, and French governments, issued in direct response to Trump's announcement in June. While German Chancellor Angela Merkel called Trump's decision to withdraw the US from the accord "extremely regrettable," French President Emmanuel Macron delivered a speech –

in English, so that no American would misinterpret him – describing it as a dangerous "mistake."

More important, governments have gone beyond words, creating facts on the ground. In October, India and the EU strengthened a partnership to develop clean-energy sources in pursuit of the Paris agreement's goals; and Nicaragua and Syria announced that they would join the agreement, making the US the only country to have spurned it. Since Trump was elected, 66 countries – including Australia, Italy, Spain, and, despite the disruption caused by its Brexit decision, the United Kingdom – have ratified the accord.

Still, while the surge in diplomatic support for the Paris agreement should be celebrated, we must not lose sight of the fundamental issue at hand: global greenhouse-gas emissions, which have effectively flatlined for the past three years. Unfortunately, this is nowhere near the level of reductions that we need.

If there was one thing that 2017 made clear, it is the devastation that awaits us if we do not do more. With unprecedented intensity and frequency, a series of hurricanes laid waste to Caribbean countries, Houston and the Gulf Coast of Texas, and large parts of Florida. In southern Europe, Australia, and the American West, wildfires tore across the countryside, claiming lives and causing extensive property damage. In South America, the Indian subcontinent, and other regions, heat waves, crop failures, and flooding reached crisis levels. And at the poles, ice sheets continued to collapse, as we witnessed most dramatically with the rupture in the enormous Larsen C Ice Shelf in Antarctica.

Sadly, Trump seems unmoved by either natural or economic realities. At this point, the US economy has twice as many jobs in renewable energy as in the coal industry, which Trump nevertheless insists on trying to prop up.

But whether Trump likes it or not, the growth of the renewable-energy sector is changing the course not just of the US economy, but of all economies worldwide. In 2017, renewables were the top form of energy to come online; and the shift to electric cars continued to accelerate, with almost every major automaker announcing plans to move away from internal combustion engines. And around the world, the threat of climate change is becoming a key driver of infrastructure investment.

At the 2017 UN Climate Change Conference in Bonn in November, China and the EU continued to fill America's shoes, by leading on global climate action. In 2018, we can expect to see more evidence of the impact of climate change, as well as significant efforts to combat it.

To be sure, these efforts will have to be much larger and more ambitious than in the past if we are to meet the goals of the Paris agreement. But, as we learned in 2017, those goals are still very much within reach. Trump or no Trump, the shift to renewable energies is irreversible, and it is driving change everywhere – including the US. PS

Laurence Tubiana, a former French ambassador to the United Nations Framework Convention on Climate Change, is CEO of the European Climate Foundation and a professor at Sciences Po, Paris.

A Truly Global Response to Climate Change

Climate action is not just about controlling global temperatures. It can also be a driver of development and poverty reduction all over the world. At the COP 23 Climate Conference in Bonn, Germany, in November, multilateral development institutions showed themselves to be more committed than ever to the urgent and central issue of supporting and financing these critical goals. ➔

Akinwumi Adesina

PRESIDENT OF THE AFRICAN DEVELOPMENT BANK.

Suma Chakrabarti

PRESIDENT OF THE EUROPEAN BANK FOR
RECONSTRUCTION AND DEVELOPMENT.

Bandar M. H. Hajjar

PRESIDENT OF THE ISLAMIC DEVELOPMENT BANK.

Werner Hoyer

PRESIDENT OF THE EUROPEAN INVESTMENT BANK.

Kundapur
Vaman Kamath

PRESIDENT OF THE NEW DEVELOPMENT BANK.

Jim Yong Kim

PRESIDENT OF THE WORLD BANK.

Jin Liqun

PRESIDENT OF THE ASIAN INFRASTRUCTURE
INVESTMENT BANK.

Luis Alberto Moreno

PRESIDENT OF THE INTER-AMERICAN
DEVELOPMENT BANK.

Takehiko Nakao

PRESIDENT OF THE ASIAN DEVELOPMENT BANK.

Today's political climate is uncertain. But climate change is not. Partnership around the world must be maintained in the global effort to achieve a smooth transition to low carbon and climate-smart development. Multilateral development institutions have never been more relevant.

Climate-smart development also makes good economic and business sense, particularly when it comes to sustainable infrastructure. We have already witnessed tremendous growth in renewable energy, creating with it new business opportunities and jobs. Many climate-smart investments can also reduce air pollution and congestion. Building resilience now saves money later. We are committed to supporting a climate-smart future.

As multilateral development institutions, we reconfirm our commitment to the Paris climate agreement. Our role is to facilitate the public and private finance that is a vital part of the climate solution.

That is why, two years after the Paris accord was successfully negotiated, we are increasingly aligning actions and resources in support of developing countries' goals. In July, the G20 Sustainability Action Plan embedded the Paris agreement in G20 policies and noted that more effective use of financing from multilateral development institutions is key to innovation and private investment in climate action.

In 2016 alone, multilateral development institutions committed over $27 billion in climate finance, and we continue to step up our work, determined to broaden the private and public finance mobilized for climate action at COP 23.

We commit to:

Deliver on the promises that we made in 2015 to increase our support for climate investments in developing countries by 2020, both from our direct financing and from our mobilization efforts.

Increase mobilization of private-sector investment by supporting policy and regulatory reforms. This includes aligning price signals, making innovative use of policy and finance instruments and, as applicable, leveraging concessional (below-market-rate) finance to help scale up public and private investment in climate projects.

Strengthen international efforts by working together and with other development finance institutions, to increase transparency and consistency in tracking climate finance tracking and reporting greenhouse-gas emissions.

Put climate change at the heart of what we do, bringing climate policy into the mainstream of our activities, and aligning financial flows to the Paris agreement.

Support countries, cities, and territories with their own climate action plans and build the conditions for an ambitious next generation of such contributions.

Work with our clients to support initiatives that protect the most climate-vulnerable areas, including small island developing states, while mobilizing more finance for developing countries to build resilience and to adapt their infrastructure, communities, ecosystems, and businesses to the consequences of climate change.

Each of these measures supports our strong commitment to the UN's Sustainable Development Goals. By pursuing them, climate action will become a key part of the international community's work to place infrastructure and the rollout of new technologies and policies for energy, water, and mobility at the core of sustainable development.

This is a serious response to a serious challenge. Climate change poses a grave threat to the natural environment, to economic growth, and to the lives of all people around the world, especially the poorest and most vulnerable.

It is fitting that this threat to national economies and to every person on earth, and the opportunity to counter it, should be tackled with the backing of multilateral development institutions. We call on others to join us in placing climate action at the center of their business, stepping up climate finance, and tracking its impact around the world. PS

Akinwumi Adesina is President of the African Development Bank.

Suma Chakrabarti is President of the European Bank for Reconstruction and Development.

Bandar M. H. Hajjar is President of the Islamic Development Bank.

Werner Hoyer is President of the European Investment Bank.

Kundapur Vaman Kamath is President of the New Development Bank.

Jim Yong Kim is President of the World Bank.

Jin Liqun is President of the Asian Infrastructure Investment Bank.

Luis Alberto Moreno is President of the Inter-American Development Bank.

Takehiko Nakao is President of the Asian Development Bank.

Saving the Environment and the Economy

EDMUND S. PHELPS
Nobel laureate economist

Every country has national problems, such as a dangerous loss of inclusion or a costly loss of growth. We learn that a solution does not happen without society's understanding of the problem and a wide desire for action.

But with climate change, all countries have a shared problem, too. And although experts have gained understanding and reached a consensus on the objectives to be sought, these goals require wider support from society than exists so far.

As everyone knows, most of the climate change started with the burning of fossil fuels brought by the industrialization that began in the late eighteenth century and has been producing rising levels of carbon dioxide ever since.

A major point is that the climate has already deteriorated to such an extent that it has become costly to society and even dangerous to life: The violence of hurricanes has risen following the rise of water temperature in the Caribbean. Air quality is deteriorating noticeably around the world. And rising sea levels are threatening many low-lying cities.

In his recent book, *Endangered Economies*, economist Geoffrey Heal surveys the array of measures, public and private, taken to block further climate change. A point introduced by Heal is that the damage – in many cases, the devastation – done to our natural world has serious consequences not only for the air and water we depend on for our existence, but also for businesses, which have relied on free natural benefits like pollination, the water cycle, marine and forest ecosystems, and more. Thus, preserving "natural capital" would raise the rate of return on capital in the business sector. Businesses would react by investing more, thus boosting productivity in the economy. And with each such boost, we could afford a greater effort that would preserve still more of the world's natural capital.

The world, then, must give up aspiring to economic growth so rapid that it is running down the world's natural capital. We want economic growth that is "green" – without damaging or destroying the environment. At the same time, we want improvement of the environment without stopping innovation and economic growth.

In a series of powerful presentations and interviews, the Columbia economist and mathematician Graciela Chichilnisky contends that mankind's survival requires that we remove the CO_2 already accumulated in the atmosphere and ensure that it stays out of the atmosphere. To cover the cost, Chichilnisky proposes a marketplace in which the captured carbon is sold for commercial use.

Another possible solution is "regenerative agriculture," such as what the biologist Allan Savory recently introduced in Patagonia.

If made profitable, these innovations could create an incentive for private actors to undertake carbon capture far beyond what a national government could afford to conduct. However, success will depend on whether "carbon farming" stays profitable even in a context of increasing supply, and thus falling prices.

We will also have to come to grips with fundamental challenges such as continuing population growth, industrialization, and weak governance. And we will have to strike a balance between fighting climate change and ensuring that most people still have lives that are worth living.

Much environmental damage is not straightforward to control.

1.

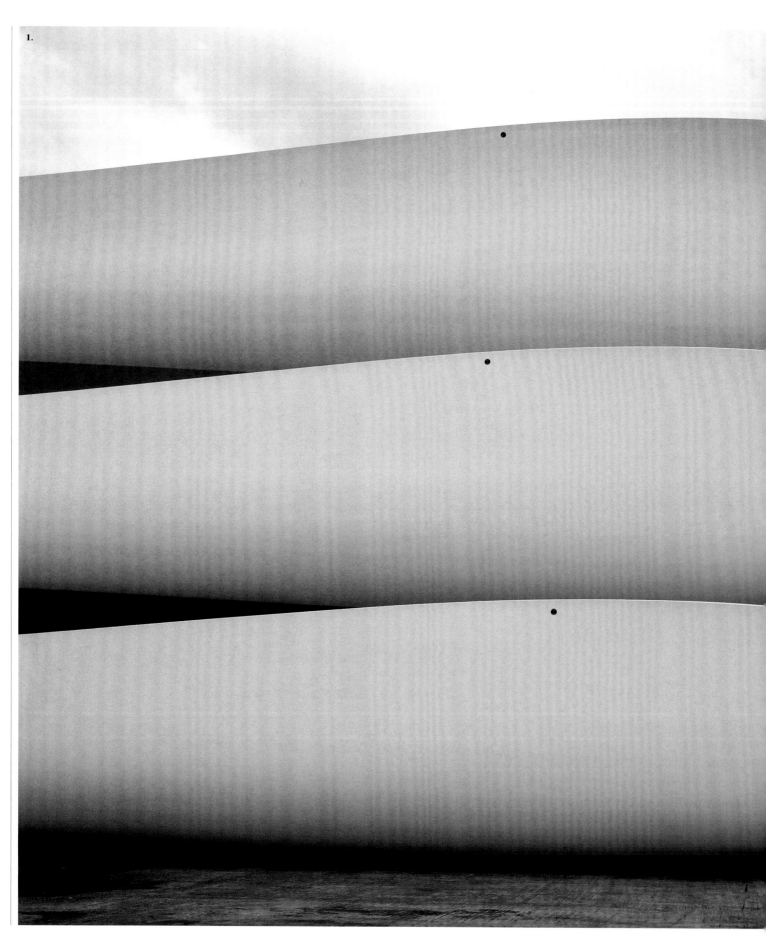

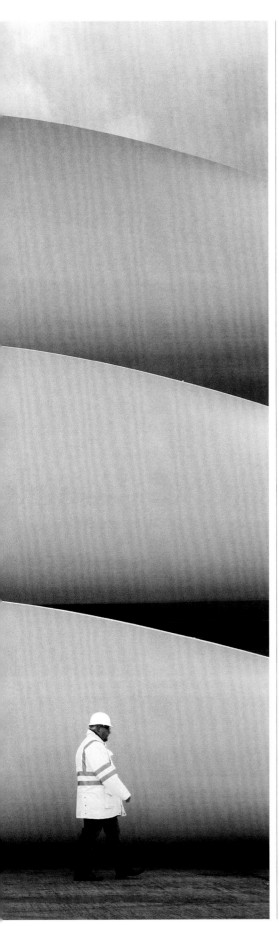

1:
A WORKER PASSES WIND TURBINE BLADES
IN BELFAST, NORTHERN IRELAND.

One might look at the growing body of research into climate change and conclude that we can rest easy: the experts have already worked out what needs to be done. But the experts themselves are not so naive. They know that businesses will not police themselves, and they recognize that much will depend on whether the profit motive can be harnessed for social good. The problem is that too many people assume that businesses, households, and policymakers will simply do what the experts recommend: that all companies – out of social pressure or threats from the state – will pay for the damage they cause; and that all governments will eventually institute carbon taxes or cap-and-trade arrangements to reduce and eventually eliminate emissions.

Another problem is that much environmental damage is not straightforward to control. Even if large public companies see fit to offset their pollution by, say, replanting rainforests in Central America, the earth has come to have a human population that is huge and still rising. This presents challenges. As the economist Dennis J. Snower showed some years ago, discrete individual activities – such as fishing, cooking on wood-fired stoves, or simply letting the water run – can contribute significantly to pollution and environmental degradation, but go largely unseen by governments, communities, and individuals. That being the case, any program to protect the environment must be based on moral suasion: to call on all individuals – not just corporations – to summon whatever sense of altruism they have and curb voluntarily their own polluting.

We will also have to confront the fact that not all governments are able to stand up to vested interests.

1.

777,000

NUMBER OF PEOPLE EMPLOYED
IN THE US SOLAR AND WIND
INDUSTRIES IN 2016.

Yet, another problem is that many countries are still undergoing industrialization. So, even if every country on the planet could reduce its *per capita* contribution to pollution, the ongoing rise in the proportion of the world's population working in countries that are now in the stage of industrializing will pull up the global average. Clearly, this demographic phenomenon will make for tough sledding as we pursue Heal's proposed measures to limit CO_2 emissions.

We will also have to confront the fact that not all governments are able to stand up to vested interests. Powerful companies can get away with violating environmental restrictions issued by the government, especially if they are a major source of income and jobs.

More difficulties arise if most people are still poor but determined to become rich – as rich as the richest countries in the West. In such a country, the government might not be ready to cut deep into carbon emissions or other pollution lest it miss its growth target. It has been estimated that 20% of the world's population accounts for 80% of the world's consumption of natural resources. Because the right to survival trumps any one country's right to ruin the environment in pursuit of growth,

the countries leading the fight against climate change will have to be tough with those that think the costs of reducing emissions are too high.

Lastly, renewable energies could pose new challenges for wages and employment in the future. According to the International Renewable Energy Agency, the US wind and solar industries have been creating jobs – employing 777,000 people in 2016 – while the coal industry has continued to shed them. But this is not a useful observation, given that employees flocking to new industries generally come from other industries, not from some vast pool of unemployed but well-suited workers. It would be absurd to think that total employment is raised by every newly arriving industry.

Economic theory implies that a new industry will expand overall employment only if its method of production is more labor-intensive than the cross-industry average. However, I have yet to see data for the renewables sector that addresses this issue, and I would not be surprised if the industry became highly capital-intensive over time.

I have long emphasized not just the material rewards of work – mainly wage rates (from the bottom up) and labor force participation rates – but also the non-material side of work (the various satisfactions that people get from the experience of work). Now that the imagination and ingenuity of our experts and engineers have helped us turn the corner, it will be important that we get back to business: to conceive of new products and methods of production, test them in the market, and strive for the new.

"Young America," Abraham Lincoln once said, "has a great passion – a perfect rage – for the 'new'." It is time for us all to be young like that again. As the project to reclaim our environment plays out and as the other international challenges are being met and resolved, also to revive an older conception of work based on exercising one's initiative and using one's creativity. The good life must again be understood as a personal voyage into the unknown, through which one might "act on the world" and "make your garden grow" – in order to be "somebody."

The worry – my worry, at any rate – is that our national economies, many of them already highly regulated in the name of stability, will become much more regulated in the name of a green economy. Yes, many regulations may be needed, but we must be careful in our efforts to save the planet that we do not strangle the sources of what makes life worth living. ᛈ

Edmund S. Phelps, *the 2006 Nobel laureate in economics, is Director of the Center on Capitalism and Society at Columbia University. His most recent book is* Mass Flourishing.

1:
A LABORER STANDS NEAR A FURNACE AT AN UNAUTHORIZED STEEL FACTORY IN INNER MONGOLIA, CHINA.

2:
EDMUND S. PHELPS.

3:
WORKERS EXAMINE A PHOTOVOLTAIC BOARD IN BAODING, CHINA.

Augmented Intelligence

STUART YOUNGS
Founder of Texture

Everybody's talking about it. Some people want it. Some people have it. Many people fear it. But what is AI? And how will it change our industry in the future?

"Artificial" intelligence. It sounds scary. Fear not, though: AI in the purists' sense – autonomous machines that think and learn – is a little way off (unless you're a tech giant).

However, key elements of AI – namely, machine learning and representation learning – are on our doorstep. And these alone will transform both the process and outcomes of our work.

First, let's reframe AI. It's not about machines taking over – they're not the enemy. This is not a contest pitting human against machine. We are partners.

Machines are objective. They don't have down days. They don't have egos. They're fast, accurate, and can operate at a scale that we can only imagine.

But machines have to be trained; and if you train your machines on garbage, what you get back will be rubbish. So quality of data becomes ever more precious in the AI age. And it's here that we see the advantage we have over machines. Machines are driven by data, which means they are not great creative or original thinkers.

This makes our relationship with AI a simple one. We have ideas; machines hone and optimize them. We create more effective work, and they constantly learn which work is effective.

So it's less about Artificial Intelligence and more about Augmented Intelligence. And it's less about data and more about tech advances in cognitive psychology, image processing, and linguistic analysis. It's this blend of innovations that will be transformational for us.

For example, we will be able to predict emotional response to content at a speed and scale that was previously unimaginable. And it will not be only positive and negative sentiment, but rather the full spectrum of emotions, from specific audiences – all at the push of a button.

This will enable us to test messaging in an instant, better marry images with text and even predict response to video.

Beyond that, machines will be able to learn a brand's tone of voice to ensure consistency and coherence at a global scale. (No more brand police surely has to be a good thing?) We'll even be able to better match digital advertising content to the context in which it's seen. (Surely this has to be a good thing, too – no more irrelevant or, worse, offensive ads chasing you around the web.)

This is not science fiction. These are all products currently being developed. And they're going to revolutionize the way we use technology in our day-to-day work.

All that said, AI will not make every campaign a success. AI will not turn a shoddy, ill-conceived campaign into a "I wish I'd thought of that" moment. But it will improve the emotional connection our content has with the audiences we want to engage.

Stuart Youngs *is a founder of Texture – a lab developing breakthrough AI for the communications industry.*

www.texture.ai

THE **MARKET** IS NOT A **DEITY.**
IT'S A **TOOL.**

OUR CHALLENGE TODAY IS TO HARNESS ECONOMIC FORCES FOR THE BENEFIT OF SOCIETY.
RISE TO THE CHALLENGE WITH US.

Institute for
New Economic Thinking

ineteconomics.org

The Glob
Econom
Risky
Recover

JOSEPH E. STIGLITZ
Nobel laureate economist

A year ago, I predicted that the most distinctive aspect of 2017 would be uncertainty, fueled by, among other things, Donald Trump's election as president in the United States and the United Kingdom's vote to leave the European Union. The only certainty, it seemed, was uncertainty – and that the future could become a very messy place.

As it turned out, although 2017 was not a particularly great year, it was far better than many had feared. Trump proved every bit as bombastic and erratic as expected. Anyone who paid attention only to his incessant tweets might think the US was teetering between a trade war and a nuclear war. Trump would insult Sweden one day, Australia the next, and then the EU – and then support neo-Nazis at home. And the members of his plutocratic cabinet rival one another in terms of conflicts of interest, incompetence, and sheer nastiness.

There have been some worrisome regulatory rollbacks, especially concerning environmental protection, not to mention the many hate-driven acts that Trump's bigotry may have encouraged. But, so far, the combination of America's institutions and the Trump administration's incompetence has meant that there is (fortunately) a yawning gap between the president's ugly rhetoric and what he has actually accomplished.

Most important for the global economy, there has been no trade war. Using the exchange rate between Mexico and the US as a barometer, fears for the future of the North American Free Trade Agreement have largely subsided, even as trade negotiations have stalled. Yet the Trump roller-coaster never ends: 2018 may be the year that the hand grenade Trump has thrown into the global economic order finally explodes.

Some point to the US stock market's record highs as evidence of some Trumpian economic miracle. I take it partly as evidence that the decade-long recovery from the Great Recession is *finally* taking hold. Every downturn – even the deepest – eventually comes to an end; and Trump was lucky to be in the White House to benefit from the work of his predecessor in setting the scene.

But I also take it as evidence of market participants' short-sightedness, owing to their exuberance at potential tax cuts and the money that might once again flow to Wall Street, if only the world of 2007 could be restored. They ignore what followed in 2008 – the worst downturn in three quarters of a century – and the deficits and growing inequality that previous tax cuts for the super rich have brought. ➡

1:
US PRESIDENT DONALD TRUMP.

2:
BRITAIN'S SECRETARY OF STATE FOR EXITING THE EUROPEAN UNION, DAVID DAVIS, AND THE EU'S CHIEF BREXIT NEGOTIATOR, MICHEL BARNIER.

3:
XI JINPING'S RE-ELECTION IN 2017.

The EU is being tested, and there are well-founded fears that it will be found wanting.

They give short shrift to the deglobalization risks posed by Trump's protectionism. And they don't see that if Trump's debt-financed tax cuts are enacted, the Fed will raise interest rates, setting off a market correction.

In other words, the market is once again showing its proclivity for short-term thinking and pure greed. None of this bodes well for America's long-term economic performance; and it suggests that while 2018 is likely to be a better year than 2017, there are large risks on the horizon.

It's a similar picture in Europe. The UK's decision to leave the EU didn't have the jolting economic effect that those who opposed it anticipated, largely because of the pound's depreciation. But it has become increasingly clear that Prime Minister Theresa May's government has no clear view about how to manage the UK's withdrawal, or about the country's post-Brexit relationship with the EU.

There are two further potential hazards for Europe. One risk is that heavily indebted countries, such as Italy, will find it difficult to avoid crisis once interest rates return to more normal levels, as they inevitably will. After all, is it really possible for the eurozone to maintain record-low rates for the foreseeable future, even as US rates increase?

Hungary and Poland represent a more existential threat to Europe. The EU is more than just an economic arrangement of convenience. It represents a union of countries with a commitment to basic democratic values – the very values that the Hungarian and Polish governments now disparage.

The EU is being tested, and there are well-founded fears that it will be found wanting. The effects of these political tests on next year's economic performance may be small, but the long-term risks are clear and daunting.

On the other side of the world, Chinese President Xi Jinping's Belt and Road Initiative is changing Eurasia's economic geography, putting China at the center, and providing an important stimulus for region-wide growth. But China must confront many challenges as it undergoes a complicated transition from export-led growth to growth driven by domestic demand, from a manufacturing economy to a service-based economy, and from a rural to an urban society. The population

is aging rapidly. Economic growth has slowed markedly. Inequality is by some accounts almost as severe as in the US, where it is the fourth-highest in the OECD (behind Mexico, Turkey, and Chile). And environmental degradation poses a growing threat to human health and welfare.

China's unprecedented economic success over the past four decades has been partly based on a system whereby broad consultation and consensus-building within the Communist Party and the Chinese state underpinned each set of reforms. Will Xi's concentration of power work well in an economy that has grown in size and complexity? A system of centralized command and control is incompatible with a financial market as large and complex as China's; at the same time, we know where insufficiently regulated financial markets can lead an economy.

But these are all essentially long-term risks. For 2018, the safe bet is that China will manage its way, albeit with slightly slower growth.

In short, as the advanced economies' post-2008 recession fades into the distant past, global prospects for 2018 look a little better than in 2017. The shift from fiscal austerity to a more stimulative stance will reduce the need for extreme monetary policies, which almost surely have had distortionary effects not just on financial markets but also on the real economy.

But the concentration of power in China, the eurozone's failure (thus far) to reform its flawed structure, and, most important, Trump's contempt for the international rule of law, his rejection of US global leadership, and the damage he has caused to democracy's standing all pose deeper risks. Indeed, they threaten not just to hurt the global economy, but also to slow what, until recently, had seemed to be an inevitable march toward greater democracy worldwide. We should not let short-run success lull us into complacency. **PS**

Joseph E. Stiglitz, a Nobel laureate in economics, is University Professor at Columbia University and Chief Economist at the Roosevelt Institute.

SHORT-TERM GAINS, LONG-TERM HAZARDS

MAURICE OBSTFELD
Chief Economist of the IMF

The year 2017 appears to be ending on a high note, with GDP growth in much of the world continuing to rise, marking the broadest cyclical upswing since the start of the decade. Throughout Europe and Asia, and in the United States and Canada, growth expectations have risen, while some important emerging economies that until recently were shrinking – for example, Brazil and Russia – have resumed growth.

Several countries continue to struggle, including many fuel exporters and low-income economies suffering from civil strife or natural disasters, especially drought. But faster recovery is benefiting roughly two-thirds of the world's population.

These developments follow years of geographically uneven, stop-and-go growth following the global crisis of 2008-2009 and the subsequent 2010-2011 rebound. As recently as early 2016, the world economy sputtered, driving the price of oil to near $25 per barrel (it is now around $60) and yielding the weakest global growth rate since the outright contraction of 2009. Thus, heading into 2018, the sense of relief among many economic policymakers is palpable.

Why has economic performance improved? While there has been a marked rise in indicators of consumer and business sentiment, and with them, investment, it would be wrong to attribute the recent upswing entirely to happenstance or "animal spirits." Fundamental factors, notably macroeconomic policies, have been at work as well.

Monetary policy has long been and remains accommodative in the largest countries. Even though the United States Federal Reserve continues to raise interest rates gradually, it has been cautious, having wisely responded to the turbulence of early 2016 by postponing previously expected rate increases. The European Central Bank has started to taper its large-scale asset purchases, but has also signaled that interest-rate increases are a distant prospect.

As a result, financial conditions have been easy, buoying both lending and asset prices worldwide. Fiscal policy in advanced economies has, on balance, shifted from contractionary to roughly neutral over the past few years, while China has provided considerable fiscal support since its growth slowed at mid-decade, with important positive spillovers to its trade partners.

Despite so much stimulus, inflation rates remain relatively low – indeed, puzzlingly so in the advanced economies – even as gaps between actual and potential GDP have narrowed or closed. Some might view the current configuration of more robust growth and low inflation as a sweet spot – the best of all possible worlds.

> **The key to improving long-run growth prospects and perceived fairness is investment in people.**

Apprenticeship programs, moreover, can save resources wasted through high youth unemployment, while counseling and retraining can prolong working lives.

For many countries, however, longer-term growth prospects are less encouraging. Aging workforces, slower productivity growth, and higher debt burdens since the crisis darken the outlook. For example, annual *per capita* growth in the advanced economies averaged 2.2% in the decade following 1995, and naturally dipped following the crisis; but even for the years between now and 2022, annual *per capita* growth will reach only 1.4%, according to International Monetary Fund projections.

Absent some unforeseen surge in productivity, the current upswing in advanced economies will inevitably moderate: growth will slow as monetary policies and financial conditions tighten, and as countries are forced to consolidate public finances strained by high government debts and burgeoning spending on pensions and health care. In turn, slower overall growth will make it harder to counter slow wage growth, especially among the unskilled, adding to the burden of inequality and resulting resentments. Many emerging-market and low-income economies will also face headwinds.

Economic policymakers throughout the world therefore face two major challenges. First, can they act to bolster output levels over the longer term? Second, can they increase their economies' resilience and inclusiveness while reducing the likelihood that the current upswing ends in an abrupt slowdown or even a new crisis?

These two challenges are closely interrelated. Today's favorable economic conditions provide a window of opportunity for policies that can meet both.

The key to improving long-run growth prospects and perceived fairness is investment in people. Educational investment increases workers' productivity and ability to navigate structural transformation, whether due to trade or technology.

Apprenticeship programs, moreover, can save resources wasted through high youth unemployment, while counseling and retraining can prolong working lives. Conversely, failure here would be destabilizing, as weak job prospects and income inequities would fuel a stronger voter backlash against multilateralism in international relations and prudent economic policies at home.

As essential as these investments are, they require fiscal outlays. To avoid inflating already-high public-debt burdens, governments will need to reform tax regimes, enhancing revenues without discouraging growth. Tax systems should be designed to increase inclusion, not least by promoting labor-force participation. And citizens will have more confidence in the system's fairness if the channels for tax avoidance used by big corporations and the rich are sealed off.

Greater economic resilience is also needed to boost confidence. As memories of the last financial crisis wane, financial instability poses an increasing threat. Many countries improved their macro-prudential frameworks after the crisis, including by raising banks' capital and liquidity. The prolonged period of low interest rates following the crisis has, however, led to a search for yield and global debt buildup that could prove problematic for some borrowers once interest rates rise.

Several economic studies, including from the IMF, suggest that even if debt booms are associated with faster growth in the short run, they often end in tears. Some countries must rein in excessive credit growth and reduce or eliminate fiscal subsidies to debt issuance, while others still need to address the bad loans left

1:
AN APPRENTICE AT
A CAR BODY PLANT.

behind by previous recessions. Countries should strengthen financial oversight as well as their international regulatory cooperation, thereby avoiding a race to the bottom in prudential policy.

Emerging and low-income economies face some challenges that resemble those in advanced economies. China's leaders, for example, have recognized the imbalances in the country's financial system and are moving to address them. But several challenges are distinct. Notwithstanding the recent uptick in commodity prices, commodity-producing countries need to diversify their economies' export mixes to support future growth.

Because the current upswing is broad, the moment is also ripe for action on a range of multilateral priorities. Probably the most urgent of these is to slow long-term climate change resulting from dependence on fossil fuels.

IMF research shows how vulnerable low-income countries are to the likely temperature increase over the rest of this century, even if the 2015 Paris climate agreement achieves its goal of holding the increase to less than 2° Celsius above pre-industrial levels. But advanced economies are vulnerable as well, including through the spillovers of political instability and mass migration originating in warmer regions. It is in their interest to embrace more ambitious emissions targets and aid low-income countries' adaptation efforts.

The bottom line is that reveries of an economic sweet spot risk lulling policymakers into a false sense of security. Current good times are most likely temporary – indeed, the forces producing this upswing may not last much longer. To make the recovery more durable, policymakers should seize the current opportunity and reform while they still can. Otherwise, the future may be closer than we think. PS

Maurice Obstfeld is Chief Economist of the International Monetary Fund.

WILL THE CENTER HOLD?

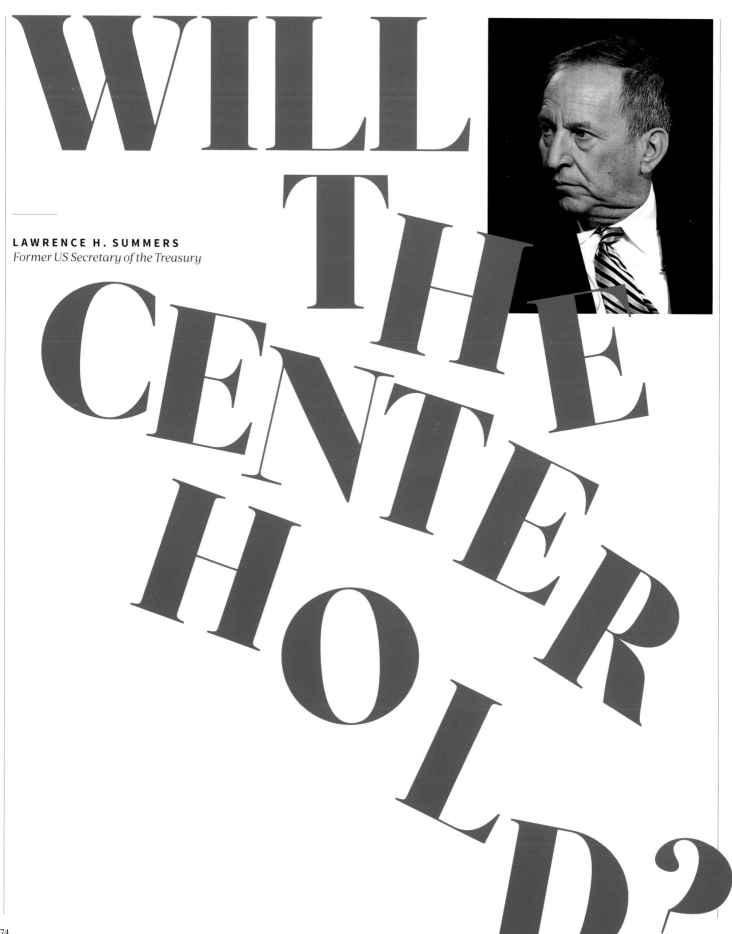

LAWRENCE H. SUMMERS
Former US Secretary of the Treasury

The most important question facing the United States – and in many ways the world – after the events of 2017 is this: Will Yeats' fearful prophecy that "Things fall apart; the center cannot hold" come true? Will it continue to seem that "The best lack all conviction while the worst are full of passionate intensity"? It is hard not to be concerned, but it is too soon to anticipate failure.

The US now has a president who regularly uses his Twitter account to heap invective on leaders of nuclear-armed states, the American news media, members of his own cabinet, and religious and racial minorities, while showering praise on those who traduce the values of democracy, tolerance, and international law.

Countries such as China, Russia, Turkey, and Saudi Arabia are more authoritarian, more nationalist, and more truculent on the world stage than they were a year ago. And then there is the surely more belligerent and possibly more erratic leader of North Korea, a country on the brink of developing the ability to deliver nuclear weapons at long range.

Europe also faced trials in 2017. Aside from the United Kingdom's decision to proceed with its withdrawal from the European Union, the far right won seats in the German Bundestag for the first time in decades, and far-right parties and candidates did better than ever in a number of European elections. In mid-November, 60,000 people marched through Warsaw demanding a "White Europe."

So there is plenty of passionate intensity. And much of it is directed at the traditions and understandings that have made the last several decades the best in human history, in terms of living standards, human emancipation, scientific and artistic progress, reduction in pain and suffering, or minimization of premature and violent death.

Will things stay together? Can some kind of center hold? Financial markets offer a remarkably optimistic view. The US stock market has broken one record after another in the year since Donald Trump's election as president, while indicators of realized stock-market volatility and of expected future volatility are at very low levels by historical standards. And some stock markets around the world have done even better.

While high equity prices and low volatility may seem surprising, they likely reflect the limited extent to which stock-market outcomes and geopolitical events are correlated. For example, Japan's attack on Pearl Harbor, the assassination of President John F. Kennedy, and the 9/11 terrorist attacks had no sustained impact on the economy. The largest stock-market movements, such as the 1987 crash, have typically occurred on days when there was no major external news.

Stock markets are buoyant because they comprise individual companies, and, to a remarkable extent this year, corporate profits have been both rising and predictable. How long this will last is difficult to judge, and there is a risk that investors are increasingly taking on leverage or pursuing strategies – such as contemporary versions of portfolio insurance – that will cause them to sell if markets decline. It is worth remembering that, looking back, markets do not appear to have been remarkably bubbly prior to the 1987 crash.

There is also the question of financial institutions' health. While major firms appear far better capitalized and far more liquid than they were prior to the crisis, market indicators of risk suggest we may not be quite as far out of the woods as many suppose. Despite apparently large increases in capital and consequent declines in leverage, it does not appear that bank stocks have become far less volatile, as financial theory would predict if capital had become abundant.

I shudder to think what a serious recession will mean for politics and policy.

1.

Financial markets are widely cited, including by US President Donald Trump, as providing comfort in the current moment. But a relapse into financial crisis would likely have catastrophic political consequences, sweeping into power even more toxic populist nationalists. In such a scenario, the center will not hold.

Beyond the kind of near-term risks that markets price, there is the question of an economic downturn. The good news is that sentiment is positive in most of the world. Inflation seems unlikely to accelerate out of control and force a lurch toward contractionary fiscal and monetary policies. Most forecasters regard the near-term risk of recession as low.

But recessions are never predicted successfully, even six months in advance. The current expansion in the US has gone on for a long time, and the risk of policy mistakes there is very real, owing to highly problematic economic leadership in the Trump administration. I would put the annual probability of recession in the coming years at 20-25%. So the odds are better than even that the US economy will fall into recession in the next three years.

The risk from a purely economic point of view is that the traditional strategy for

battling recession – a reduction of 500 basis points in the federal funds rate – will be unavailable this year, given the zero lower bound on interest rates. Nor is it clear that the will or the room for fiscal expansion will exist.

This means that the next recession, like the last, may well be protracted and deep, with severe global consequences. And the political capacity for a global response, like that on display at the London G-20 Summit in 2009, appears to be absent as well. Just compare the global visions of US President Barack Obama and UK Prime Minister Gordon Brown back then with those of Trump and Prime Minister Theresa May today.

I shudder to think what a serious recession will mean for politics and policy. It is hard to imagine avoiding a resurgence of protectionism, populism, and scapegoating. In such a scenario, as with another financial crisis, the center will not hold.

But the greatest risk in the next few years, I believe, is neither a market meltdown nor a recession. It is instead a political doom loop in which voters' conclusion that government does not work effectively for them becomes a self-fulfilling prophecy. Candidates elected on platforms of resentment delegitimize the governments

they lead, fueling further resentment and even more problematic new leaders. Cynicism pervades.

How else can one explain the candidacy of Roy Moore for a US Senate seat? Moore, who was twice dismissed for cause from his post on the Alabama Supreme Court, and who is credibly charged with sexually assaulting teenage girls when he was in his 30s, could enter the US Senate as many of his colleagues look the other way.

If a country's citizens lose confidence in their government's ability to improve their lives, the government has an incentive to rally popular support by focusing attention on threats that only it can address. That is why in societies pervaded by anger and uncertainty about the future, the temptation to stigmatize minority groups increases. And it is why there is a tendency for officials to magnify foreign threats.

We are seeing this phenomenon all over the world. Russian President Vladimir Putin, Turkish President Recep Tayyip Erdoğan, and Chinese President Xi Jinping have all made nationalism a central part of their governing strategy. So, too, has Trump, who has explicitly rejected the international community in favor of the idea that there is only a ceaseless

struggle among nation-states for competitive advantage.

When the world's preeminent power, having upheld the idea of international community for nearly 75 years, rejects it in favor of *ad hoc* deal making, others have no choice but to follow suit. Countries that can no longer rely on the US feel pressure to provide for their own security. America's adversaries inevitably will seek to fill the voids left behind as the US retrenches.

Changes in tax, regulatory, or budget policy can be rescinded – albeit with difficulty – by a subsequent administration. A perception that the US is no longer prepared to stand up for its allies in the international community is much less reversible. Even if the US resumes its previous commitments, there will be a lingering sense that promises broken once can be broken again. And once other countries embark on a new path, they may be unable or reluctant to reverse course.

So, will the center hold? Will the international order remain broadly stable? The answer will depend on the Trump administration's choices and other governments' responses. But as other countries watch America, they will

be looking at more than its president, especially as his popular approval continues to decline. That is why it is more important than ever that all Americans proclaim their continuing commitment to democracy and prosperity at home and to leadership of the global community. **PS**

Lawrence H. Summers, US Secretary of the Treasury (1999-2001) and Director of the US National Economic Council (2009-2010), is a former president of Harvard University, where he is currently University Professor.

1:
STEPHEN BANNON.

2:
RUSSIAN PRESIDENT VLADIMIR PUTIN AND TURKISH PRESIDENT RECEP TAYYIP ERDOĞAN.

77

Will Monetary Policy Trigger Another Financial Crisis?

ALEXANDER FRIEDMAN
Chief Executive Officer of GAM

Former US President Ronald Reagan once quipped that, "The nine most terrifying words in the English language are: I'm from the government and I'm here to help." Put another way, policymakers often respond to problems in ways that cause more problems.

Consider the response to the 2008 financial crisis. After almost a decade of unconventional monetary policies by developed countries' central banks, all 35 OECD economies are now enjoying synchronized growth, and financial markets are in the midst of the second-longest bull market in history. With the S&P 500 having risen 250% since March 2009, it is tempting to declare unprecedented monetary policies such as quantitative easing (QE) and ultra-low interest rates a great success.

But there are three reasons for doubt. First, income inequality has widened dramatically during this period. While negative real (inflation-adjusted) interest rates and QE have hurt savers by repressing cash and government-bond holdings, they have broadly boosted the prices of stocks and other risky financial assets, which are most commonly held by the wealthy. When there is no yield in traditional fixed-income investments such as government bonds, even the most conservative pension funds have little choice but to pile into risk assets, driving prices even higher and further widening the wealth divide.

According to a recent Credit Suisse report, America's richest 1% now own about half

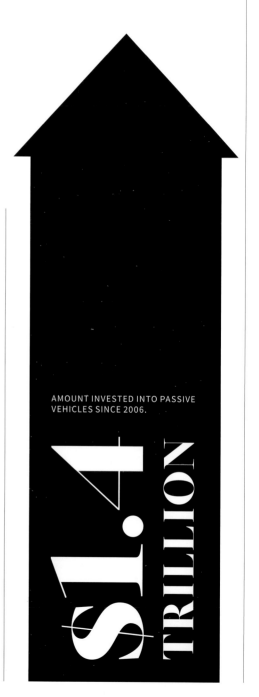

AMOUNT INVESTED INTO PASSIVE VEHICLES SINCE 2006.

$1.4 TRILLION

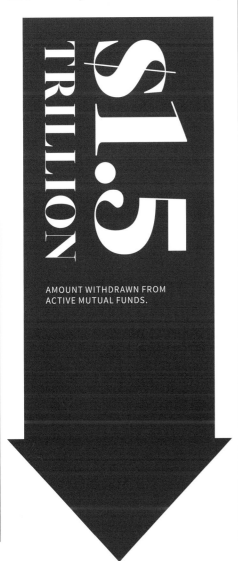

the national wealth in investment assets such as stocks and mutual funds, while the bottom 90% of Americans derive the majority of their wealth from their homes – an asset class that took a big hit from the recession. In fact, the wealthiest Americans now own nearly as large a share of national wealth as they did in the 1920s. And at the global level, the top 1% owns half of all assets, and the top 10% owns 88%.

Moreover, though monetary stimulus has allowed companies to borrow and refinance at record-low costs, they have felt little pressure to raise wages. In the US, real wages in 2017 were just 10% higher than they were in 1973. And, despite the size and duration of monetary stimulus, central banks have consistently fallen short of their inflation targets. Today's missing inflation may reflect deflationary pressure from demographic aging; globalization and the availability of low-cost labor abroad;

$1.5 TRILLION

AMOUNT WITHDRAWN FROM ACTIVE MUTUAL FUNDS.

the spread of automation and labor-saving technologies; energy-sector productivity gains that neutralize price increases; or other factors. Whatever the case, the net effect of low inflation in the developed world is a less stable social fabric, and an expanding wealth gap that fuels populism.

A second reason to worry about the policy response over the past decade is that the rising tide of risk assets, driven by QE, has supercharged passive investing. This trend has introduced a host of new risks. Since the crisis, markets have been tightly correlated, dispersion rates have been exceptionally low, and investing has largely followed a risk-on, risk-off pattern, all of which is perfect for low-cost passive investing to outperform active management. Accordingly, since January 2006, investors have put more than $1.4 trillion into passive vehicles such as index funds, while withdrawing $1.5 trillion from active mutual funds.

Yet even as investment managers have launched thousands of new products to meet rising demand, the environment that supported passive strategies has begun to change. For starters, central banks are, or will soon be, normalizing monetary policy by rolling back their bond purchases. With dispersions between assets and within asset classes on the rise, the performance pendulum has already started to swing back toward active management. And at the same time, the huge accumulation in passive investments over the past decade has heightened the potential for capital misallocation and asset-price distortions, while raising concerns about fiduciary duties of care and other systemic issues.

A third reason for caution is that central banks have yet to reverse fully their unconventional policies and unwind their giant balance sheets. If managing the financial crisis and rolling out unprecedented policies seemed difficult, just wait for what has to come next: withdrawal of unprecedented levels of liquidity from the economy. The balance sheets of the US Federal Reserve, the European Central Bank, the Bank of Japan, the Bank of England, and the Swiss National Bank have swelled to a combined $15.5 trillion – a fourfold expansion since the end of 2007.

The great unwinding that awaits the world economy will introduce a slew of major new risks. The size of central

banks' balance sheets is a function of the demand for money, and of the supply created by monetary expansion. Even if central bankers can gauge the demand for money accurately enough to ensure a stable balance-sheet adjustment in 2018 and beyond, additional challenges will remain. For example, if market participants, having never witnessed such a monetary normalization, were to misread central bankers' intentions, they could end up reprising the 1994 bond-market crash. With new leadership at the Fed, effective communication will be more of an uncertainty.

Moreover, pension funds, having taken on ever more risk in their search for yield, will have to reconcile lower future market returns and increased volatility with the needs of an older population. In 2015, one-eighth of the global population was age 60 or over. According to the United Nations, that ratio will increase to one-sixth by 2030, and to one-fifth by 2050.

If pension funds cannot meet their obligations in the future, governments will have to step in to provide a safety net. And yet total government debt as a share of global GDP has increased at an annual rate of over 9% since 2007, putting it at around 325% of GDP; as a result, the bond market may not be there to back-stop indebted governments. If pensions and governments in advanced economies cannot provide for the elderly, social instability is sure to follow.

As we enter 2018, we must hope that central banks will be as adept at reducing their role in the global economy as Reagan was in restoring the market to the center of the US economy. Success will depend on two factors. First, central banks will have to resist politicization, and maintain their independence and extraordinary technical know-how. And, second, they will need to pursue the great normalization gradually and avoid abrupt moves. Of course, to do that, they will have to maintain the tricky balance of sustained moderate growth and low inflation that has characterized 2017. **PS**

Alexander Friedman, Chief Executive Officer of GAM, was Global Chief Investment Officer of UBS, Chief Financial Officer of the Bill & Melinda Gates Foundation, and a White House fellow during the Clinton Administration.

HOW INEQUALITY WORKS

ANGUS DEATON
Nobel laureate economist

I nequality has been named as a culprit in the populist incursions of 2016 and 2017. But what is inequality, and what role does it play in inhibiting or encouraging growth, or in undermining democracy? Does inequality kill, say, by driving people to suicide or to "deaths of despair"? Or is inequality a necessary evil that we must tolerate at certain levels?

These are questions I am often asked. But, truth be told, none of them is particularly helpful, answerable, or even well posed. Inequality is not so much a *cause* of economic, political, and social processes as a *consequence*. Some of these processes are good, some are bad, and some are very bad indeed. Only by sorting the good from the bad (and the very bad) can we understand inequality and what to do about it.

Moreover, inequality is not the same thing as unfairness; and, to my mind, it is the latter that has incited so much political turmoil in the rich world today. Some of the processes that generate inequality are widely seen as fair. But others are deeply and obviously unfair, and have become a legitimate source of anger and disaffection.

In the case of the former, it is hard to object to innovators getting rich by introducing products or services that benefit all mankind. Some of the greatest inequalities today are a consequence of industrial and health revolutions that began around 1750. Originally, these processes benefited just a few countries in northwest Europe. But they have since improved living conditions and health outcomes for billions of people around the world. The inequalities stemming from

these advances – both within and between countries – are beneficial and fair, and a key feature of progress generally.

On the other hand, getting rich by bribing the state for special favors is clearly unfair, and rightly resented. Many in the United States – more so than in Europe – automatically regard capitalist or market outcomes as fair, and government action as arbitrary and unfair. They object to government or university-sponsored programs that seem to favor particular groups, such as minorities or immigrants.

This helps to explain why many white working-class Americans have turned against the Democratic Party, which they view as the party of minorities, immigrants, and educated elites. But another reason for growing public discontent is that median real (inflation-adjusted) wages in the US have stagnated over the past 50 years.

There are two different explanations for the divergence between median and top incomes, and it matters a great deal which one is correct. The first attributes it to impersonal and unstoppable processes such as globalization and technological innovation, which have devalued low-skill labor and favored the well educated. ⊙

Although globalization and technological change have disrupted traditional work arrangements, both processes have the potential to benefit everyone.

$1 TRILLION

ANNUAL US EXPENDITURE ON EXCESSIVE HEALTHCARE COMPARED TO OTHER RICH NATIONS.

$8,000

THIS EQUATES TO AROUND $8,000 PER AMERICAN FAMILY.

The second explanation is more sinister. It holds that median-income stagnation is actually the direct result of rising incomes and wealth at the top. In this account, the rich are getting richer at the expense of everyone else.

Recent research suggests that there is some truth to the second story, at least in the US. Although globalization and technological change have disrupted traditional work arrangements, both processes have the potential to benefit everyone. The fact that they have not suggests that the wealthy have captured the benefits for themselves. It will take much more work to determine which policies and processes are holding down middle- and working-class wages, and by how much, but what follows is a preliminary list.

First, health-care financing is having a disastrous effect on wages. Because most Americans' health insurance is provided by their employers, workers' wages are essentially paying for profits and high salaries in the medical industry. Every year, the US wastes a trillion dollars – about $8,000 per family – more than other rich countries on excessive health-care costs, and has worse health outcomes than nearly all of them. Any one of several European financing alternatives could recoup those funds, but adopting any of them would trigger the fierce resistance of those now profiting from the *status quo*.

A related problem is increasing market consolidation in many sectors of the economy. As a result of hospital mergers, for example, hospital prices have risen rapidly, but hospital wages have not, despite a decades-long shortage of nurses. Increasing market concentration is probably a factor underpinning slow productivity growth, too. After all,

it is easier to reap profits through rent-seeking and monopolization than through innovation and investment.

Another problem is that the US federal minimum wage – currently at $7.25 per hour – has not increased since July 2009. Despite broad public support, raising the minimum wage is always difficult, owing to the disproportionate influence that wealthy firms and donors have in Congress.

Making matters worse, more than 20% of workers are now bound by non-compete clauses, which reduce workers' bargaining power – and thus their wages. Similarly, 28 US states have now enacted so-called "right-to-work" laws, which forbid collective-bargaining arrangements that would require workers either to join unions or pay union dues. As a result, disputes between businesses and consumers or workers are increasingly settled out of court through arbitration – a process that is overwhelmingly favorable to businesses.

Yet another problem is outsourcing, not just abroad, but also within the US, where businesses are increasingly replacing salaried or full-time workers with independent contractors. The food servers, janitors, and maintenance workers who used to be a part of successful companies are now working for entities with names like AAA-Service Corporation. These companies operate in a highly competitive low-wage industry, and provide few or no benefits and little opportunity for advancement.

The earned income tax credit (EITC) has provided a boost in living standards for many low-paid US workers. But, because it is available only to those who work, it puts downward pressure on wages in

1:
VETERANS AND FAMILY
MEMBERS WAIT IN LINE
TO ATTEND A CAREER FAIR.

a way that unconditional benefits, such as a basic-income grant, would not.

Unskilled immigration also poses a problem for wages, though this is controversial. It is often said that immigrants take jobs that Americans do not want. But such statements are meaningless without some reference to wages. It hard to believe that low-skilled Americans' wages would have remained as low as they did in the absence of inflows of unskilled immigrants. As the economist Dani Rodrik pointed out 20 years ago, globalization makes demand for labor more elastic. So, even if globalization does not reduce wages directly, it makes it harder for workers to get a pay raise.

Another structural problem is that the stock market rewards not just innovation but also redistribution from labor to capital. This is reflected in the share of profits relative to GDP, which has grown from 20% to 25% over the same period that median wages have stagnated. The increase would be even higher if executive salaries were counted as profits rather than wages.

The final problem on our preliminary list is political. We have entered a period of regulatory bonfires. The Consumer Financial Protection Bureau, despite having uncovered major scandals, is now under threat, as is the 2010 Dodd-Frank legislation, which introduced measures to prevent another financial crisis. Moreover, President Donald Trump has indicated that he wants to eliminate a rule requiring money managers to act in their clients' best interest. All of the deregulatory "reforms" currently being proposed will benefit capital at the expense of workers and consumers.

The same is true of US Supreme Court rulings in recent years. The court's decision in *Citizens United v. FEC*, for example, gave wealthy Americans and even corporations the ability to spend almost unlimited amounts to support candidates and engineer legislative and regulatory outcomes that work in their favor.

If this account of stagnant median wages and rising top wages is correct, then there may be a silver lining to our era of inequality, because it means that the US's dysfunctional labor market is not an irremediable consequence of unstoppable processes such as globalization and technological change.

Broadly shared progress can be achieved with policies that are designed specifically to benefit consumers and workers. And such policies need not even include redistributive taxation, which many workers oppose. Rather, they can focus on ways to encourage competition and discourage rent-seeking.

With the right policies, capitalist democracy can work better for everyone, not just for the wealthy. We do not need to abolish capitalism or selectively nationalize the means of production. But we do need to put the power of competition back in the service of the middle and working classes. **PS**

***Angus Deaton**, the 2015 Nobel laureate in economics, is Presidential Professor of Economics at the University of Southern California and Professor of Economics and International Affairs at Princeton University's Woodrow Wilson School of Public and International Affairs.*

EAST ASIA'S RISING STAR

SRI MULYANI INDRAWATI
Finance Minister of Indonesia

At the World Bank Group's Annual Meetings in Washington, DC, in October, there was notable optimism in anticipation of an upswing in the global economy. The International Monetary Fund's latest World Economic Outlook projects that global growth will accelerate to 3.6% in 2017, and to 3.7% in 2018. Not surprisingly, investment, trade, industrial production, and business and consumer confidence have continued to increase in several key economies and regions. ➡

1.

1:
INDONESIAN PRESIDENT
JOKO WIDODO.

2:
SRI MULYANI INDRAWATI.

3:
RESIDENTS OF JAKARTA'S TEBET
DISTRICT PLAY FIRE FOOTBALL.

Indonesia intends to capitalize fully on this upswing. In 2017, it consistently posted a respectable growth rate of around 5% – better than most emerging economies – owing to increased investment and consumption, and a recovery in exports, partly owing to the pick-up in commodity prices. In fact, exports are becoming an increasingly reliable third engine of growth for the country.

Better still, Indonesia's macroeconomic indicators are sound. The country is experiencing solid growth in new jobs and real wages, and low and stable inflation of around 4%. Moreover, food prices are steady, consumer confidence is strong, interest rates are low, and the exchange rate has remained consistent. Domestic

and foreign direct investment have been picking up, too, thanks to increased infrastructure spending.

These positive trends have added momentum to ongoing reforms. After all, the best time to mend one's roof is when the sun is shining. Accordingly, President Joko Widodo's government is pushing ahead with key measures that will create a strong foundation for higher long-term competitiveness. And alongside structural reforms, we are pursuing prudent fiscal and monetary policies, with our sights set well beyond the horizon.

The proof of Indonesia's progress is in the pudding. Indonesia has gained growing international recognition, with three major rating agencies having issued the

country an investment-grade credit rating. According to an OECD/Gallup poll, 80% of Indonesians have confidence in the national government – the highest among all countries surveyed.

Moreover, Indonesia's standing in the World Bank's "Ease of Doing Business" ranking has skyrocketed 34 places since the current government took office in 2014. Owing to its improved business and investment climate under President Joko Widodo's leadership, Indonesia has been named a top-ten reformer.

Toward the end of 2017, the Indonesian parliament approved a robust 2018 national budget, which aims to boost confidence further, increase productivity, and enhance the country's competitiveness. For the past three years, the government has pushed hard to invest in the future by closing the country's infrastructure and human-capital gaps. The new budget will continue that work by increasing investments in both areas to unprecedented levels.

Even more than our natural resources and strategic location, our people are the most precious assets of all. As the world's fourth most populous country, Indonesia has a large and vibrant young workforce that will fuel inclusive growth well

into the future. Indonesian millennials are more connected, creative, and confident than any previous generation. They are our future entrepreneurs, job creators, professionals, civil-society leaders, and taxpayers. And they are already competing vigorously in the digital economy, where technological innovations will continue to introduce new opportunities and challenges.

The next generation will have to start preparing today for the jobs and opportunities of tomorrow. To that end, the government has placed special emphasis on investments in human capital. More than 20% of the 2018 national budget is allocated for education and vocational training; and another 5% is dedicated to the health sector.

Furthermore, the government is providing support for the country's poorest and most vulnerable communities. Through social safety nets, cash transfers, cash-for-work programs, and other innovations, we are lifting people out of the vicious cycle of poverty. The government's flagship "Indonesia Pintar" education program will ensure that around 20.3 million school-age children stay in school. The "Indonesia Sehat" health initiative is expanding access to basic

health services for the masses. And large-scale microcredit programs have been introduced to kick start local economies.

With more than 17,000 islands spread over three time zones, Indonesia is the world's largest archipelago. Fortunately, ongoing investments in infrastructure will leave the economy more interconnected than it has ever been. As logistical costs fall and efficiency improves, we will likely see the emergence of new growth centers beyond the main islands.

Lastly, the government is working hard to strengthen Indonesia's institutions. We have introduced a comprehensive tax-reform plan to make collection more effective, and to broaden the tax base. And we are taking steps to ensure financial inclusion, and to improve trade and investment policies, all of which will fuel competitiveness.

Any businessperson or investor who overlooks Indonesia risks missing out on the opportunities offered by a global economic success story. As a member of the G20, Indonesia is the largest economy in Southeast Asia, and on its way to becoming the fifth largest economy in the world by 2030. When Indonesia thrives, everyone benefits.

Indonesians are doing their part to contribute to the dynamism of East Asia. As the Indonesian economy continues to gain momentum, so, too, will the current government's efforts to establish a strong foundation for the future. **PS**

Sri Mulyani Indrawati is Finance Minister of Indonesia and Chair of the World Bank Group's Development Committee.

AFRICA, the BUSINESS Deal OF THE CENTURY

CÉLESTIN MONGA
*Vice President and Chief Economist
of the African Development Bank*

As experts speculate about global growth in 2018 and beyond, few pay much attention to Africa. Those who do often stress that the continent remains home to the highest proportion of poor people in the world, or that large numbers of young people are fleeing their countries in search of security and opportunity. Even the more optimistic economic forecasters tend to refer to Africa in negative terms, advocating a latter-day Marshall Plan, not as a catalyst for business partnerships and growth, but as a new form of humanitarianism.

$500 BILLION

ANNUAL TAX AND OTHER FISCAL REVENUES FOR AFRICA.

10X

THIS AMOUNTS TO MORE THAN TEN TIMES THE FOREIGN AID THE CONTINENT RECEIVES PER YEAR.

To be sure, Africa's GDP *per capita* stands at only $2,000 per year, and the region has the lowest proportion of wage earners (around 20%) in the world. Persistent poverty, together with climate change, are aggravating high rates of unemployment and underemployment. Most of the labor force is still trapped in low-productivity, subsistence activities, with the fiscal capabilities of many states depending heavily on declining commodity prices.

While structural transformation is taking place, it is happening very slowly. Africa accounts for just 1.9% of global value-added in manufacturing – a share that hasn't risen in decades. Moreover, Africa's population of 1.2 billion is growing fast, at 2.6% per year, with the youth bulge – 70% of Africa's population is under the age of 30 – putting pressure on governments suffering from weak planning and managerial capacity.

Nonetheless, such talk about "Africa" is misplaced. There are many "Africas." The continent comprises 54 countries, with widely varying economic performance. In 2016, *per capita* gross national income (GNI) ranged from $280 in Burundi to nearly $15,500 in Seychelles.

War-torn and conflict-affected African countries such as South Sudan rank high on the list of Africa's worst economic performers. But the continent also boasts some of the world's fastest-growing economies: Côte d'Ivoire, Ethiopia, Rwanda, Tanzania, and Senegal. And Africa has about 30 middle-income countries, whose combined middle class – estimated at some 300 million people – is growing fast.

Yet the world's advanced economies are not paying sufficient attention to this dynamic emerging Africa, which means that they are missing out on the opportunities that the continent has to offer. At the same time, rich countries have excess savings, which encourage excessive risk-taking by yield-hungry bankers – behavior that eventually creates financial bubbles. By contrast, poor countries have investment deficits, which are constraining growth and perpetuating economic and social misery in Africa – problems that eventually lead to poverty, conflicts, political instability, and mass migration of skilled and unskilled labor.

It doesn't have to be this way. The discrepancy between global excess savings and the profitable investment opportunities in the developing world – especially in Africa – reflects the fact that intermediation is not taking place. ➡

WORKERS TOIL AT A COPPER SMELTER
IN NDOLA, ZAMBIA.

1.

The substantial sums of private financing dwarf the total volume of official development assistance, which amounted to $135 billion in 2015 ($45 billion of which went to Africa). The estimated $7 trillion held by sovereign wealth funds is another potential global source of investment financing.

Developed-country investors should be channeling some of this financing to poor countries, particularly in Africa, which now face investment deficits, despite offering profitable opportunities. A study by McKinsey & Co. shows that the rate of return on foreign investment is higher in Africa than anywhere else in the developing world. Yet only a fraction of global foreign direct investment (FDI) flows – projected to resume growth in 2017, and to surpass $1.8 trillion in 2018 – are likely to go to Africa.

One key reason for this is the perception that Africa's business environment is poor. But despite its generally weak tax-collection record, Africa generates tax and other fiscal revenues of $500 billion annually – more than ten times the foreign aid the continent receives per year. And $60 billion of the $432 billion in officially recorded remittances that went to developing countries in 2015 went to Africa.

1:
WORKERS POLISH DIAMONDS AT A FACTORY IN GABORONE, BOTSWANA.

2:
FEMALE AGRO-DEALER IN KISUMU, KENYA.

Yet the continent spends more than $300 billion annually to import goods that it could produce cheaply and competitively within its borders, if its industrialization strategies focused on promoting industries with a competitive advantage. Capital flight is rampant in some countries. And ineffective management of foreign exchange and government revenue leads to substantial opportunity costs.

Creating a financing framework for channeling excess savings from the global North into profitable investment opportunities in the global South would benefit everyone: African countries in need of financing, private investors searching for opportunities, and advanced economies seeking new sources of export demand. The key would be to target Africa's most competitive, labor-intensive industries, supporting them not just with money, but also through institutions such as development banks, industrial parks, and agencies that provide certification and quality infrastructure.

With appropriate policies, industrialization in Africa would help to raise productivity, including by spurring technological progress and innovation, while creating higher-skill jobs in the formal sector,

It sounds like a bonanza-in-waiting – and so it is.

thereby boosting average incomes and domestic consumption. It would also promote linkages between the services and agricultural sectors; between rural and urban economies; and among consumers, intermediates, and capital goods industries. And, by making the prices of manufactured exports less volatile and susceptible to long-term deterioration than those of primary goods, industrialization would help countries escape dependence on commodity exports.

The United Nations Industrial Development Organization (UNIDO) has estimated that increasing manufacturing's share of GDP in Africa and Least-Developed Countries could lead to an aggregate positive investment shock of about $485 billion, and to an increase in household consumption of about $1.4 trillion. According to UNIDO research, *per capita* investment would rise by $66 for every additional percentage point in manufacturing's share of GDP in Africa, while *per capita* consumption would increase by $190.

This rise in investment and consumption would boost demand for imported capital and consumer goods from other regions of the world, most notably the G20 economies. Increased production of capital and consumer goods would activate several multiplier effects, generating further demand for intermediate inputs, higher employment, and faster income growth.

It sounds like a bonanza-in-waiting – and so it is. Smart investors will not ignore it. PS

Célestin Monga is Vice President and Chief Economist of the African Development Bank Group.

2.

CENTRAL BANKS' YEAR OF RECKONING

RAGHURAM G. RAJAN
Former Governor,
Reserve Bank of India

Since 2008, central banks in industrial countries have deviated from ordinary monetary policymaking in a variety of ways. They've tried to persuade the public through "forward guidance" that interest rates would stay low for extended periods of time. And they've deployed various programs such as long-term refinancing operations (LTROs), the Securities Markets Program (SMP), and quantitative easing (QE) in pursuit of various goals. ➡

More recently, central banks have also introduced negative interest rates and – from the Bank of Japan (BOJ), which has always been at the forefront of innovation – yield-curve targeting. And some central banks have resorted to unconventional but well-known policies such as direct exchange-rate targeting.

But now, with most major central banks apparently seeking to normalize monetary policy, we should ask why these extraordinary measures were used and whether they worked. Looking forward, we should ask what effect phasing them out will have, and whether their use raises long-term concerns. By addressing these questions, central bankers will be better prepared to grapple with future crises.

Was It Necessary?

It is worth recalling that markets were clearly broken after the 2007-2008 financial crisis. With credit flows frozen, it was understandable that central banks would go to great lengths to stabilize financial markets, whether the mortgage-backed securities market in the US or the sovereign-bond market in Europe.

But a second reason for central banks to intervene was to affect yields or prices. This was a more adventurous objective, given that central banks typically manage prices only indirectly, by raising or lowering the policy interest rate, not through direct intervention. But when the policy rate reached the zero lower bound, central bankers deemed it necessary to affect prices on a variety of long-term securities, sometimes by targeting a particular class of security in the hope that the effect would spread across classes.

A third reason for central-bank intervention was to signal a commitment to preferred monetary policies. For example, if a central bank announced a program to purchase government securities, the implication was that it would not tighten monetary policy while the program was in effect. Regardless of the program's stated intent, its corollary effect was to signal "low-for-long" interest rates.

Central banks have cited all of these justifications for pursuing occasionally aggressive – or innovative – monetary policies. But as an ex-central banker, I would include another reason, one that monetary authorities rarely mention:

they are prisoners of their inflation-targeting mandate.

When central banks began setting a target band for inflation in the 1980s and 1990s, they were really focused on the upper limit. Few central bankers expected that the problem with inflation-targeting regimes would be the lower bound, and that they would be struggling to move inflation up into the band rather than down into it. They are now trapped by a mandate they do not necessarily know how to achieve.

The BOJ has been attempting to push inflation up for close to a decade and a half. During this time, many central bankers from around the world have been happy to tell BOJ officials, "It's very easy. Here's how you do it." But when these same central bankers have found themselves facing low inflation, they have come to realize that things aren't so simple.

One reason is that nobody really knows how to dislodge the public's expectation of low inflation, which seems to fuel low inflation itself. Even the nuclear option of dropping "helicopter money" on the economy will fail if the people it lands on think the central bank piloting the mechanism is deranged. Fearing a future day of reckoning, people may simply stuff the cash into a mattress or into their savings accounts, instead of spending it.

In such an environment, central bankers really do have to worry that if they admit to having "no policy instruments left," the public's inflation expectations will collapse. Accordingly, they will always claim to have one more inflation-boosting bazooka up their sleeve, which they hope they will never have to bring out, let alone fire.

Though we have not seen a negative disinflationary spiral, which central bankers fear most, inflation has remained stubbornly low. Central bankers have thus constantly upped the ante on monetary innovation – that is, new instruments that might theoretically boost inflation – even though the ineffectiveness of their instruments has become increasingly apparent.

According to this logic, when QE has run its course, central banks must move to negative interest rates. And when negative interest rates prove insufficient, they must move to yield-curve targeting.

Few central bankers expected that the problem with inflation-targeting regimes would be the lower bound, and that they would be struggling to move inflation up into the band rather than down into it.

At each stage, when a policy instrument proves increasingly ineffective, they have to roll out something new so that they aren't seen as being complacent. Not providing an alternative would suggest that they have given up hope – and that everyone else should, too. That would virtually guarantee failure to achieve their mandate.

Did It Work?

This brings us to the second question: Did any of these innovative instruments work? In terms of stabilizing markets, yes, some policies seem to have been quite effective, either because a deep-pocketed player came in to buy securities, or because central banks put their weight behind markets and said, "We're going to be here to make sure they function." Spreads for periphery sovereign credit in Europe were widening rapidly until European Central Bank President Mario Draghi announced in July 2012 that the ECB would do "whatever it takes" to

preserve the euro. That statement alone had a magical effect on markets.

But to the extent that these interventions were also intended to achieve inflation mandates, then, no, they have not worked – at least not yet. The United Kingdom has experienced a Brexit-induced currency depreciation and consequent inflation, which cannot really be credited to the Bank of England's actions. The Fed is probably the closest to its target of about 2% PCE (personal consumption expenditure) inflation, but it is struggling to get there, despite a tight labor market. Other central banks remain wider of the mark.

Of course, central bankers would tell us that it's only a matter of time before they hit their targets, and that their actions prevented a collapse of inflation expectations. Perhaps so. It's possible that expectations haven't spiraled downward in Japan and some other countries because central banks have repeatedly indicated that they are committed to their mandate and won't give up. But it's also possible

A more fundamental question is whether central banks should offload their balance sheets at all.

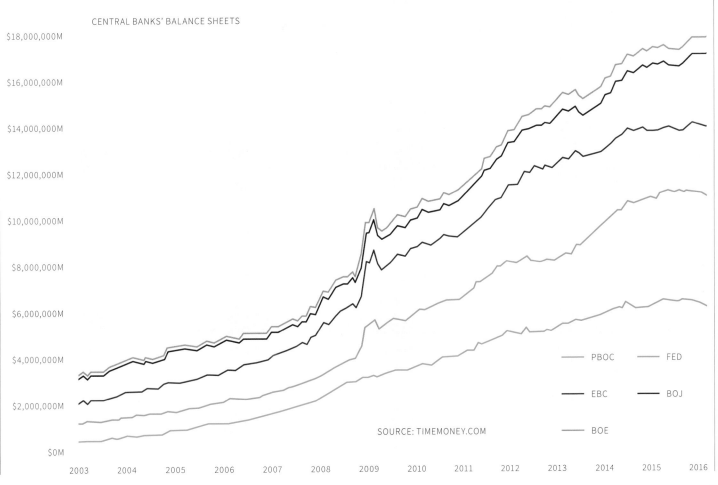

CENTRAL BANKS' BALANCE SHEETS

SOURCE: TIMEMONEY.COM

PBOC — FED — EBC — BOJ — BOE

1:
HARUHIKO KURODA, GOVERNOR
OF THE BANK OF JAPAN.

2:
MARIO DRAGHI, PRESIDENT OF
THE EUROPEAN CENTRAL BANK.

that inflation has stabilized at a low level for other reasons.

Whether unconventional policies have had a direct effect on long-term interest rates (other than through signaling) also remains unclear. The evidence that they have is mixed. Some effects can be seen within a narrow timeframe and for a narrow class of instruments; but as soon as you expand your view, unconventional policies' influence becomes much harder to discern. Or, to take one example, when the Fed buys US Treasury bonds, it has an effect on Treasuries. But it is much harder to make the case that it also has an effect on the entire spectrum of bonds. Complicating matters further, it is even more difficult to establish any link between unconventional policies and investment or consumption in the real economy.

In sum, central banks' extraordinary policies have probably had a positive effect in terms of repairing markets and signaling long-term accommodative monetary policies. But their effect on real activity remains uncertain.

Safe to Let Go?

What happens when policies are reversed? The nice thing about expectations is they get front-loaded. We may have already seen what happens when a central bank changes signals: during the "taper tantrum" of 2013, a general sense that the Fed might terminate QE and start raising interest rates triggered market turmoil and quickly drove interest rates up.

Markets have since stabilized, but it remains to be seen if unconventional policies' effects on financial-asset prices will be reversed when the policies are. As central banks start shrinking their balance sheets in 2018, longer-term bonds will be returned to the market, and the market's holdings of excess reserves will be extinguished. Bond issuers will need to find more private buyers, but private buyers will have funds to buy more bonds. As this asset swap takes place, long-term interest rates can be expected to rise somewhat. And if markets are worried about the eventual stock they'll have

1.

to absorb, the rise in interest rates could be rather abrupt.

Thus far, the Fed has advertised a measured pace of balance-sheet reduction, and the market seems to have taken this quite well. With much of the signaling behind us, one hopes that the bonds that are effectively dropped from the Fed balance sheet will be absorbed without sharp changes in bond prices, and only modest rises in long-term interest rates over time.

A more fundamental question is whether central banks should offload their balance sheets at all. Harvard University's Jeremy C. Stein, Robin Greenwood, and Samuel G. Hanson contend that central banks should keep their balance sheets relatively large, because doing so creates safe, short-term instruments that the financial world lacks. When the private sector tries to meet the demand for short-term liabilities, they argue, it typically assumes too much risk, which then haunts the entire system.

But there are at least two reasons why central banks shouldn't make big balance sheets permanent. For starters, to do so

would be to take on liquidity management as a public service. The private sector's inadequacy in performing this role during the financial crisis is not a good enough reason for central banks to perform it permanently. It is well known that publicly provisioned insurance-like services typically result in overreliance by the private sector and underpricing by the public sector. And, as my University of Chicago colleague Douglas Diamond and I have shown, privately provisioned liquidity services may have many additional benefits that are not always acknowledged in the public debate.

Moreover, large central-bank balance sheets introduce political risks. As Charles Plosser, a former president of the Federal Reserve Bank of Philadelphia, explains, when a central bank expands its balance sheet and uses it in ways that are not entirely tied to monetary policy, it exposes itself to political pressures. ➲

By prompting a search for yield, easy monetary conditions have reduced risk premia for all types of assets.

2.

For example, if the government needs, say, $500 billion for infrastructure spending, it will see little reason not to pressure the Fed to convert some of its holdings into infrastructure assets worth $500 billion. Central bankers in emerging markets are used to such requests. And while they usually politely refuse, they also understand that it is harder to say no when maintaining a large balance sheet that is already disconnected from conventional monetary policy.

Long-term Risks?

Finally, there is the question of unconventional monetary policies' long-term unintended effects on risk-taking in advanced economies, capital flows to and from emerging markets, and central-bank independence generally.

By prompting a search for yield, easy monetary conditions have reduced risk premia for all types of assets. But, as Claudio Borio and William White of the Bank for International Settlements have

2:
FEDERAL RESERVE
CHAIR NOMINEE
JEROME POWELL.

3:
THE BANK OF JAPAN,
TOKYO.

warned, this accelerates the financial cycle. Moreover, the promise of bountiful liquidity has increased leverage, both explicit and implicit, because borrowers, betting on continued access to funding, view taking on further debt as a low-cost endeavor. This suggests that the financial system is becoming more fragile, which helps to explain why some central banks are considering tightening monetary policy despite remaining far from their inflation targets.

One important example of how accommodative monetary policies contribute to financial fragility is their effect on emerging markets, where yield-seeking capital pours in when major central banks slash their policy rates, and then flees from those markets when monetary policies are tightened. The 2013 "taper tantrum" was calamitous for some emerging markets because they could not cope with the large, sudden capital outflows that it fueled.

A common analogy for foreign capital is that it is like a houseguest whom emerging markets should welcome. And, for the most part, they do. But foreign capital often comes *en masse*, and then departs *en masse* without much warning. Like any host, emerging markets would love

1:
MARK CARNEY,
GOVERNOR OF THE
BANK OF ENGLAND.

3.

to know when a huge crowd of guests expects to arrive, and when it intends to leave, so that they can plan accordingly. When capital bases its decision to come or go on what happens far away, it behaves like a very bad guest.

Cross-border bank flows are especially problematic. According to a recent study by Falk Bräuning of the Federal Reserve Bank of Boston and Victoria Ivashina of the Harvard Business School, when monetary policy tightens, cross-border bank flows quickly retreat from emerging markets, owing to the short maturity on bank loans. Unlike bonds sold by foreign holders, which can be picked up by domestic investors, a reduction in lending by foreign banks may not be offset. In the absence of additional lending by local banks, emerging-market companies often experience a credit squeeze.

So far, emerging markets have learned to muddle through episodes of substantial capital-flow reversal, at some cost to themselves. But there is an urgent debate to be had about the responsibility the world's major central banks bear when these spillovers occur.

What Next?

One final question concerns the role of central banks' domestic mandates in encouraging the kind of extraordinary policies we have seen in recent years. In the past, central banks have essentially said, "Give us a mandate, and don't place constraints on how we achieve it." But while this formula may have worked fine when the primary problem was high inflation – and when central banks' primary instrument was the policy rate (and some marginal tweaks to liquidity) – it no longer works when the problem is low inflation.

Far-reaching operational freedom without a practical scientific understanding of how to achieve the mandate is a dangerous combination for central banks. They have come under intense pressure to innovate; and, at the same time, there are few assets they cannot buy, and even fewer borrowers they cannot fund.

When ostensible monetary policies increasingly have a fiscal component, central banks can end up in the business of anointing winners and punishing losers. It is then only a matter of time before politicians start asking why

central banks have so much freedom. While doing whatever it takes to achieve their mandate, central banks may have inadvertently exposed themselves to closer political scrutiny and greater risks to their independence and power.

By doing so much to make up for political inaction at the start of the 2008 financial crisis, central bankers inserted themselves into the political limelight. They are heroes, certainly, for stepping in to mitigate the crisis. But politicians do not like powerful unelected heroes. With their PhDs, exclusive jargon, and secretive meetings in far-flung places like Basel and Jackson Hole, central bankers are the quintessential rootless global elite that populist nationalists love to hate. And that was true even before central banks started to tighten monetary policy.

Central bankers would of course prefer to avoid any discussion of their function and mandate. But, rather than waiting and hoping for the public spotlight to move somewhere else, they would be better off conducting a sober assessment of their policies over the last few years. It is incumbent upon monetary authorities to devise a mandate that is both reasonable and achievable, and to establish a set of actions that are permissible in achieving the mandate. Otherwise, 2018 will be just the beginning, rather than the end, of a brave new era for monetary policy. **PS**

Raghuram G. Rajan, *Governor of the Reserve Bank of India from 2013 to 2016, is Professor of Finance at the University of Chicago Booth School of Business.*

Can Economic Policy Solve Economic Problems?

JASON FURMAN
Professor, Harvard University

The past year has witnessed several attacks, including a few near misses, on the rules-based global order that has undergirded prosperity in the world's advanced economies and the rapid growth of many emerging economies. A lively debate has ensued about whether the fundamental cause of such populist attacks is economic or cultural.

I suspect the answer is a bit of both, especially because cultural explanations raise the question of why now, whereas economic explanations provide a ready answer: the significant slowdown of income growth.

1:
JASON FURMAN, DISCUSSING THE CURRENT ECONOMIC OUTLOOK.

A tougher question is what can be done about it. The challenge we face consists in the disconnect between the economic aspirations of the discontented and the policy tools we have at our disposal to meet them. And in some cases, the tools themselves may be politically counterproductive.

Still, we must try, because surveys of life satisfaction reveal some disturbing trends. Life satisfaction in the United States, as measured by the General Social Survey, peaked in 1990 and has been largely trending down, even as household incomes have risen (albeit tepidly). Other major economies have also experienced declining levels of self-reported wellbeing, including Italy, where Pew's measure of life satisfaction peaked in 2002, and France as well.

President Donald Trump won the 2016 election partly by promising to address the drivers of these trends – promises that neither he nor anyone else could keep. He promised to restore manufacturing jobs, even though manufacturing employment is falling worldwide as machines replace humans, propelling record production without commensurate job creation.

Similarly, Trump promised to restore the coal industry, which has also been declining for decades, not only for some of the same technological reasons, but also because of the fall in the price of natural gas and, to a much lesser degree, increased regulation of coal-based energy. More broadly, his promise of substantial job creation, wage gains, and economic growth of 4% or more flew in the face of deep factors, like demographic trends and slow productivity growth worldwide, that are at the root of today's economic challenges.

The right policy agenda is one that would foster stronger, more inclusive growth. Although the details vary from country to country, they generally include improving education, increasing infrastructure investment, expanding trade, reforming tax systems, and ensuring that workers have an adequate voice in their economic futures.

But I worry that in advanced economies, all of these policies combined would make only a small dent in today's problems. Developing countries can undergo large swings in growth as a result of major policy and institutional changes – witness China's transition to a market economy,

India's reforms to end the license raj, or economic liberalization in Latin America. But advanced economies are all growing at very similar rates, and nothing in the last several decades suggests that structural policies can have a major impact on medium- and long-term growth (in certain circumstances, short-run demand policies can make a big difference).

If advanced economies did everything right, their growth rate might increase by, say, 0.3 percentage point. That is certainly worth doing; much of economic policy is about finding ways to add tiny increments to the growth rate. But I find it implausible that our politics will change radically if the median US or French household gets an extra $1,800 after a decade.

Similarly, we should be making a much more robust effort to reduce inequality. In some countries, that means strengthening workers' bargaining power – higher minimum wages and stronger unions would be a good start – while tackling issues that weaken it, like employer collusion and restraints on employees' ability to change jobs.

There has to be a better answer than just lying to people about what our policies are capable of accomplishing.

Policies that promote competition and reduce inefficient rents also have an important role to play. This includes more vigorous antitrust enforcement and efforts to reduce entry barriers, for example, by giving people ownership of their personal data. But, again, the plausible impact of such policies would fall well short of overcoming people's concerns with inequality and slow income growth.

Some other policies are economically sensible, but may be politically counterproductive. For example, while I strongly agree with the widespread

view that a robust social safety net is needed to protect the "losers" of globalization and market-based competition, I worry that creating one may be as likely to weaken as to reinforce social cohesion.

In the US, the 2010 Affordable Care Act ("Obamacare") was the largest expansion of the social safety net in almost 50 years, and it is hard to imagine another as large in the next 50 years. But increased funding for health insurance and the greatly reduced chance of becoming uninsured have not dramatically changed US politics or alleviated concerns about job losses due to trade. If anything, the Affordable Care Act may have increased polarization, given that some of what fuels populism is the resentment felt by those who perceive government benefits as going to others at their expense.

Nonetheless, such economic policies are the right steps to take, and they just might help defuse a little of the anxiety. But we must also be humble about our understanding of which solutions could address our current economic problems, particularly the need to promote higher levels of employment.

In fact, the solution to our political problems, in 2018 and beyond, may lie not in any new policies or materially changed circumstances, but in finding better ways to communicate about the challenges we face, the efforts being made to address them, and the inherent limits that confront all policymakers. There has to be a better answer than just lying to people about what our policies are capable of accomplishing. PS

Jason Furman, *Professor of the Practice of Economic Policy at the Harvard Kennedy School and Senior Fellow at the Peterson Institute for International Economics, was Chairman of President Barack Obama's Council of Economic Advisers from 2013-2017.*

Rediscо
Public
Wealth
Creatio

overing

MARIANA MAZZUCATO
Professor, University College London

At the cusp of the new year, a decades-old debate among economists is heating up again: Does austerity help or hurt economic growth? Broadly speaking, the debaters fall into two camps: conservatives who call for limited public spending, and thus a smaller state; and progressives who argue for greater investment in public goods and services such as infrastructure, education, and health care.

Of course, reality is more complex than this simple demarcation implies, and even orthodox institutions such as the International Monetary Fund have come around to the view that austerity can be self-defeating. As John Maynard Keynes argued back in the 1930s, if governments cut spending during a downturn, a short-lived recession can become a full-fledged depression. That is exactly what happened during Europe's period of austerity after the 2008 financial crisis.

And yet the progressive agenda cannot be just about public spending. Keynes also called on policymakers to think big. "The important thing for Government is not to do things which individuals are doing already," he wrote in his 1926 book *The End of Laissez Faire,* "but to do those things which at present are not done at all." In other words, governments should be thinking strategically about how investments can help shape citizens' long-term prospects.

The economic historian Karl Polanyi went even further in his classic book *The Great Transformation,* in which he argued that "free markets" themselves are products of state intervention. In other words, markets are not freestanding realms where states can intervene for good or ill; rather, they are *outcomes* of public – not only private – action. ➡

TWO TECHNICIANS
INSIDE A NASA SPACE
SHUTTLE EXTERNAL
TANK, 1980S.

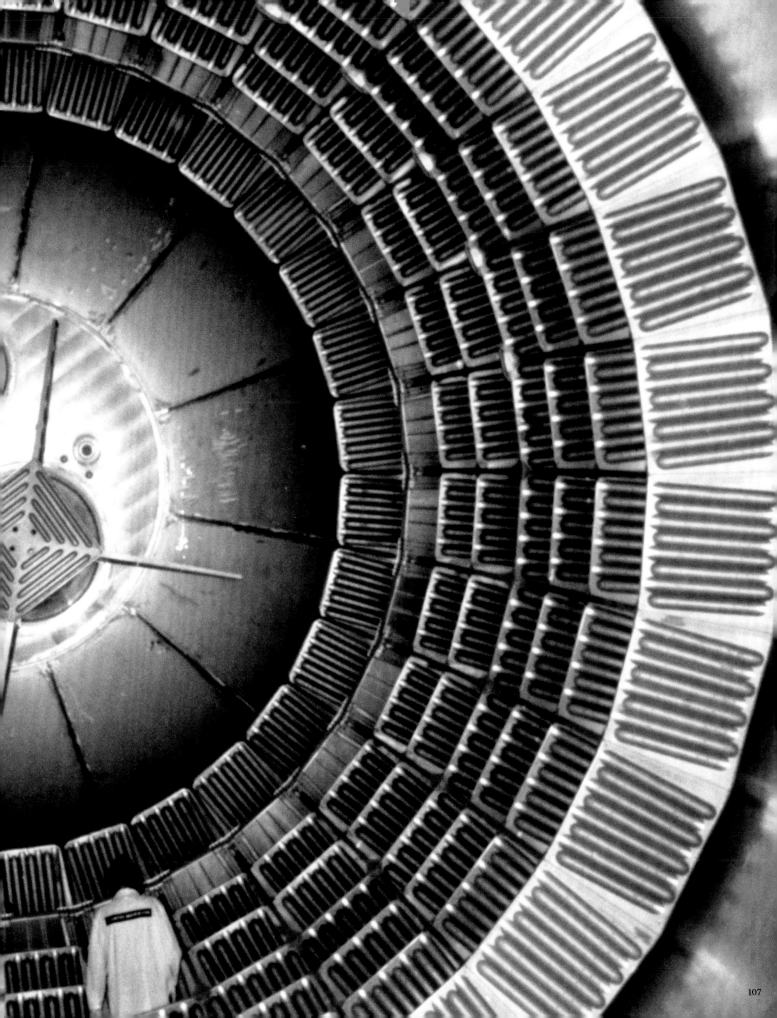

Businesses that make investment decisions and anticipate the emergence of new markets understand this fact. Top managers, many of whom see themselves as "wealth creators," take courses in decision sciences, strategic management, and organizational behavior. They are encouraged to take risks, and to fight against inertia.

But if value is created collectively, those who pursue a career in the public sector should also be taught how to think like risk takers. As it stands, they aren't. Instead, public policymakers and civil servants have come to regard themselves not as wealth or market creators, but at best, as market fixers, and at worst, as impediments to wealth creation.

This difference in self-conception is partly the result of mainstream economic theory, which holds that governments should intervene only in cases of "market failure." The state's role is to establish and enforce the rules of the game; ensure a level playing field; fund public goods such as infrastructure, defense, and basic research; and devise mechanisms to mitigate negative externalities such as pollution.

When states intervene in ways that exceed their mandate to correct market failures, they are often accused of creating market distortions, such as by "picking winners" or "crowding out" the private sector. Moreover, the emergence of "new public management" theory, which grew out of "public choice" theory in the 1980s, led civil servants to believe that they should take up as little space as possible, fearing that government failures might be even worse than market failures.

This thinking has caused many governments to adopt accounting mechanisms from the private sector, such as cost-benefit analysis, or to outsource functions to the private sector altogether, all in the name of efficiency. But this approach has not only failed to achieve its goals; it has undermined confidence in public institutions, and left them ill equipped to work with businesses to confront twenty-first-century challenges such as climate change and health-care provision for aging populations.

It was not always like this. In the postwar period, two US government agencies, NASA and the Defense Advanced Research Projects Agency (DARPA), created what would later become the Internet. Both agencies were founded in the 1950s, and were given ample funding and clear goals. Their mission-oriented approach allowed them to attract top talent, and their staff

1:
SCHOOL CHILDREN
USING A BBC COMPUTER
TERMINAL, 1987.

2:
BRITISH BROADCASTING
CORPORATION HEADQUARTERS.

3:
MARIANA MAZZUCATO SPEAKING
AT THE CEE INNOVATOR SUMMIT.

were told to think big and take risks.

Similarly, the US Advanced Research Projects Agency-Energy (ARPA-E), set up in 2009, has been responsible for significant innovations in the field of renewable energy, particularly in battery storage. The National Institutes of Health (NIH) has funded the development of many blockbuster drugs.

In the United Kingdom, the BBC's ambitious computer literacy project in the 1980s led to its investment in the Micro computer. Procurement of that device's parts enabled companies like Advanced RISC Machines, later renamed Arm, to scale up and become national powerhouses.

Today, the opposite is happening, with many mission-oriented public institutions being weakened. NASA increasingly has to justify its existence in terms of immediate economic value, rather than the pursuit of bold missions. The BBC is also evaluated according to increasingly narrow metrics, which may justify investments in high-quality content, but fail to support public value creation independent of the format.

Public value does not mean simply redistributing existing wealth or correcting issues affecting public goods.

Instead, it means co-creating value in different spaces. When mission-driven public-sector actors collaborate to tackle large-scale problems, they co-create new markets affecting both the rate of growth and its direction.

But co-creating value and directing growth require experimentation, exploration, and trial and error. It cannot work if civil servants are too risk-averse, owing to fears that a failed project might become front-page news, or are demotivated, owing to the expectation that successes will be interpreted as the work of the private sector. While market fundamentalists heaped criticism on the US government for funding the solar startup Solyndra, which eventually failed, they never mention the fact that the Tesla S, now a major success, received roughly the same amount of public support.

In this intellectual climate, it has become much easier for politicians to call for public-sector downsizing than to defend public-sector risk taking. Not surprisingly, US President Donald Trump has targeted ARPA-E, and congressional Republicans routinely threaten the public broadcaster PBS. In the UK, the BBC's prestige has not insulated it from years of fierce attacks.

The debate about growth in 2018 must include a focus on promoting risk-taking and experimentation. Such an approach can reawaken the progressive agenda, making all actors feel like they are in the driver's seat and preventing that narrow group of self-acclaimed wealth creators from simply extracting value. And it will generate a more dynamic conversation within civil society on which missions might be the best ones to bet on together. **PS**

Mariana Mazzucato is Professor in the Economics of Innovation and Public Value and Director of the Institute for Innovation and Public Purpose at University College London.

AGILE GOVERNANCE FOR A FRACTURED WORLD

KLAUS SCHWAB
*Founder and Executive Chairman
of the World Economic Forum*

As the Fourth Industrial Revolution continues to reshape the global
political economy, many are grasping for ideas about how to effect
positive systemic change. In a world where technology is both
a disrupter and the driving force of progress, the best approach
may be to apply lessons from technology to policymaking itself.
Policymakers, like start-ups, must look for more ways
to iterate what works and abandon what doesn't. ➔

To any observer of world affairs, it is clear that after a relatively long period of unprecedented peace and prosperity, and after two decades of increasing integration, openness, and inclusiveness, the pendulum is now swinging back toward fragmentation, nationalism, and conflict.

Indeed, the post-world order has already fractured in many ways. Ambitious multilateral trade agreements have fallen apart after key stakeholders walked away. Unprecedented global cooperation on climate change, embodied in the 2015 Paris climate accord, is being undermined. Separatist movements are becoming more vocal, as sub-national communities look for sources of identity that will reestablish a sense of control. And the president of the United States has indicated that he will pursue national self-interest above all else, and that other national leaders should do likewise.

These developments follow decades of globalization, which ushered in an astonishing period of progress across many dimensions, from global health and national incomes to inequality between countries. But today's fragmentation is not about sterile statistics. Rather, it is a visceral reaction to forces that have driven a wedge between economics and politics. In the space between, there is now tension; but there is also an opportunity to push for cooperation and shared progress.

The underlying economic drivers of integration remain powerful. The revolution in information and communication technologies (ICT) has drawn people from around the world closer together; changed the relationship between individuals and their communities, employers, and governments; and set the stage for a new period of economic and social development unlike anything that has come before. And yet the human drive for freedom – the chance to build a life of meaning and achievement for oneself and one's community – remains undiminished.

At the same time, there has been a political backlash against the economic

Many of those who have gotten the diagnosis right have gotten the prescription wrong.

1:
US PRESIDENT DONALD TRUMP.

1.

and technological forces of change. Power has been won by those promising to protect traditional identities and slow or reverse change, rather than accommodate it. For such politicians, the narrative is straightforward: the system is rigged against those without power or influence; and alien forces are complicating what were once simpler but more satisfying lives.

Of course, no one denies that a technology-driven global economy creates imbalances, or that greater efficiency is often achieved without greater fairness. The system that produced the past few decades of growth has emphasized the rights of shareholders over other stakeholders, thus concentrating wealth and locking out those without capital. More open trade has brought about a shift in employment patterns between and within countries. And now that a new wave of technological change is poised to overwhelm existing economic and social structures, the nature of work itself is changing.

Still, many of those who have gotten the diagnosis right have gotten the prescription wrong. For starters, none of the overarching technological and economic forces at work today can be regulated away at the national level. When the forces driving the global economy are larger than any one country or stakeholder, the pursuit of narrow, selfish interests simply cannot work. In the Fourth Industrial Revolution, policies must account for the global, regional, and inter-sectoral industrial systems that are shaping our world, and all stakeholders – whether in government, business, or civil society – have no choice but to act together, through new, innovative forms of collaboration.

The formula for building inclusive societies is well known: invest in education, reduce barriers to social and economic mobility, and encourage competition. But, as always, the devil is in the details, and one size does not fit all. Whereas some countries will need more training or wage insurance, others might have a need for minimum-guaranteed-income schemes and measures to narrow gender gaps. Government, business, and civil society must work together to experiment in these and many other areas; and citizens need reasons to believe that their leaders are acting for the common good.

The pendulum will not swing back toward collective progress on its own.

To that end, policymakers should heed the lessons of the technology sector. Given the complexity of modern economic and social systems, the outcome of a single action can hardly be predicted with certainty. An invaluable trait for any effective organization, then, is agility. Policymakers should be asking themselves when to act, and when to discontinue an action. And they should craft policy experiments with clearly discernible outcomes, so that they can determine whether a policy has worked or should end.

This kind of dynamism defines the technical and creative economy, where a start-up that is not prepared to pivot when necessary won't be around for long. Those who are successful understand clearly what they want to achieve, and they reach their goals by quickly adapting to changing conditions.

Moreover, the technology sector teaches us that collaboration between stakeholders is the best way to tap into effective talent and create an enabling, risk-taking environment. Under perennially unpredictable circumstances, leaders must be willing to adapt, explore, learn, and adjust endlessly.

Leadership in a fractured world means looking beyond the current discord to a new, shared future. It requires the courage to try something novel, with the knowledge that it might fail. We have no choice but to take such risks. The pendulum will not swing back toward collective progress on its own. We must push it, by showing that stakeholder collaboration is still possible, even in a fractured world. **PS**

Klaus Schwab is Founder and Executive Chairman of the World Economic Forum.

The World's Opinion Page

Project Syndicate was established in the early 1990s as an initiative to assist newly independent media in post-communist Central and Eastern Europe. Expansion to Western Europe, Africa, Asia, and the Americas quickly followed, as publishers worldwide sought access to the views of leading thinkers and policymakers on the day's most important global issues.

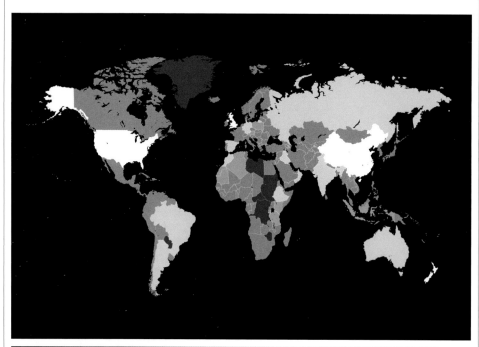

1   *PROJECT SYNDICATE'S* NETWORK OF MEMBER PUBLICATIONS   13

> **If *Project Syndicate* did not exist, we would have to invent it.**

ANNE-MARIE SLAUGHTER
President and CEO of the think tank New America.

Our rapid growth has been guided by rigorous editorial independence and a simple credo: all people – wherever they live, whatever their income, and whatever language they use – deserve equal access to the highest-quality analysis, from a broad range of perspectives, of the events, trends, and forces shaping their lives.

Project Syndicate thus provides an invaluable global public good: ensuring that news media in all countries, regardless of their financial and journalistic resources – and often in challenging political environments – can offer readers original, engaging, and thought-provoking commentary by the world's leading innovators in economics, politics, health, technology, and culture.

Without *Project Syndicate*, most of the publications we serve would be unable to secure comparable content. *Project Syndicate's* unparalleled range and caliber of opinion, our ability to provide analysis of breaking news, and our commitment to focusing minds on complex topics driving the news – development, the Middle East, Africa, and sustainability, among many others – now benefits some 300 million readers of 476 media outlets in 154 countries.

Project Syndicate
The Year Ahead 2018

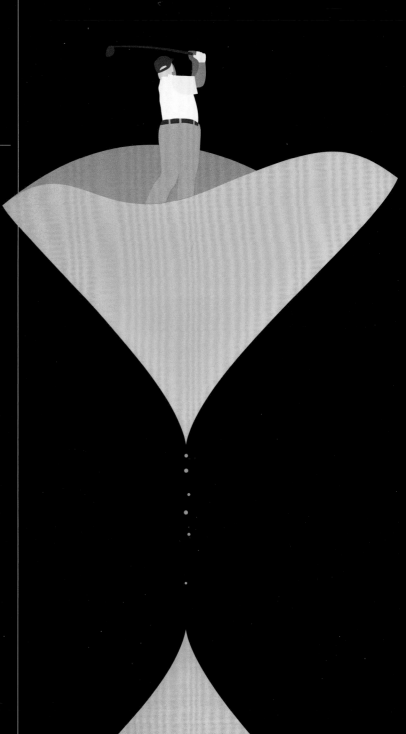

Project Syndicate

Designed by Texture
www.texture.ai